ESSAYS AND STUDIES
1976

ESSAYS AND STUDIES
1976

BEING VOLUME TWENTY-NINE OF THE NEW SERIES
OF ESSAYS AND STUDIES COLLECTED FOR
THE ENGLISH ASSOCIATION

BY E. TALBOT DONALDSON

JOHN MURRAY

FIFTY ALBEMARLE STREET LONDON

Printed in Great Britain by
Cox & Wyman Ltd, London, Fakenham and Reading

0 7195 3307 4

Contents

I

Chaucer's Use of Nicholas of Lynn's Calendar

SIGMUND EISNER

I

NICHOLAS of Lynn, a Carmelite friar who flourished at Oxford in the late fourteenth century, is the author of a still unpublished Calendar which Chaucer uses in *The Canterbury Tales* and mentions in *The Treatise on the Astrolabe*.[1] Nicholas is not garrulous about himself. He identifies himself as a Carmelite brother at Oxford, least and unworthy (*minimus et indignus*) among readers of sacred theology. He says that in 1386 he composed for the meridian of Oxford a calendar which was to run from 1387 through 1462. Written to replace a just-expired calendar composed by Walter of Elvedene, Nicholas's Calendar was dedicated to the most illustrious prince, Lord John, King of Castile and Leon, and Duke of Lancaster, that is, John of Gaunt.

There is very little solid information about Nicholas. Richard Hakluyt[2] in the sixteenth century quotes two authorities concerning a voyage supposedly made by Nicholas long before he composed his Calendar. The first, Gerard Mercator,[3] cites one James Cnoyen, who claims to have received his information from the descendant of a colonist left by King Arthur on an island in the far north. The story is that in 1360 an unidentified English Franciscan

---

[1] I am engaged in editing the Calendar of Nicholas of Lynn for the Chaucer Library, under the general editorship of Professor Robert E. Lewis of Indiana University. All citations to Chaucer are from F. N. Robinson, ed., *The Works of Geoffrey Chaucer*, 2nd ed., 1957. The abbreviation *CT* is used for *The Canterbury Tales*. All lines are numbered according to Robinson's edition.

[2] Richard Hakluyt, *Voyages*, I, Everyman's Library, No. 264 (London, 1907), pp. 99–101.

[3] Mercator's own statement appears in *Mercator's Atlas* (Amsterdam, 1636, reprinted Amsterdam, 1968), p. 44.

friar, who was a mathematician and who possessed an astrolabe, travelled to the northern islands, had an adventure with a whirlpool, described what he saw, and used his astrolabe to measure altitudes, presumably of the North Star, in order to establish his latitude. The second authority, the mathematician John Dee, writes of an Oxford friar who sailed from Lynn (since 1537: King's Lynn), wrote a travel book known as the *Inventio Fortunata*, and presented the book to King Edward III of England. Hakluyt himself identifies the friar as 'Nicholas De Linna'. This story is repeated in the *DNB*,[1] where Hakluyt's identification is ascribed to Hakluyt alone and not necessarily to fact.

Both the facts and the suppositions about Nicholas were repeated by Thomas Tanner in 1748,[2] R. T. Gunther in 1923,[3] and others.[4] None took Hakluyt's conjectures very seriously. M. C. Seymour, however, does; he states that he owns a fragment of the *Inventio Fortunata* which describes 'what is now Long Island'.[5] A. B. Emden quotes the sixteenth-century John Bale, who refers to Nicholas as '*philosophus, cosmographus, et astronomus inter omnes sui temporis celeberrimus*'.[6] Carolyn Spurgeon also quotes Bale and his source John Leland, who say that Nicholas was Chaucer's teacher at Oxford.[7] John Pits in 1613 and Richard Beatniffe in 1786 wrote of Chaucer's great respect for Nicholas.[8]

---

[1] *Dictionary of National Biography*, XL (London, 1892), 418. Hereafter abbreviated *DNB*.

[2] Thomas Tanner, *Bibliotheca Britannico-Hibernica* (London, 1748), p. 546.

[3] R. T. Gunther, *Early Science in Oxford*, II (London, 1923, reprinted 1967), 62–3.

[4] Lynn Thorndike, *A History of Magic and Experimental Science during the First Thirteen Centuries of Our Era*, III (New York, 1938), 523–4. George Sarton, 'The Mysterious Arctic Traveller of 1360, Nicholas of Lynn?', *Isis*, XXIX (1938), 98–9. Aubrey Diller, 'The Mysterious Arctic Traveller of 1360. Nicholas of Lynn', *Isis*, XXX (1939), 277–8. George Sarton, *Introduction to the History of Science*, III (Washington, 1927–48, reissued 1947–50), 1501.

[5] M. C. Seymour, *The Metrical Version of Mandeville's Travels* (London, 1973), p. 126.

[6] A. B. Emden, *A Biographical Register of the University of Oxford to A.D. 1500*, II (Oxford, 1958), 1194.

[7] Carolyn Spurgeon, *Five Hundred Years of Chaucer Criticism and Allusion, 1357–1900*, III (Cambridge, 1925), 13, 21, 22, 26.

[8] Ibid., II, 63; I, 483.

A recent speculation concerning Nicholas must be mentioned. In his excellent study, *Chaucer at Oxford and at Cambridge*,[1] Professor J. A. W. Bennett suggests that Nicholas of Lynn could be the mysterious 'Leyk', whom Dr Derek J. Price discovered in Peterhouse (Cambridge) MS 75.9 by using an ultra-violet light. Dr Price thought that 'Leyk' might be either an error for the name [John of] Linières or a transliteration of an Arabic name.[2] Professor Bennett says that 'Leyk' might also be an error for 'Lynn', and cites Bodleian MS Laud 662 as mentioning Nicholas as 'Nicholas de Leuka'. I must respectfully disagree with Professor Bennett. In MS Laud Miscellaneous 662, folio 1r, appears the name 'Nicholas de Lenea'. It is not possible to read this name as 'Leuca' unless one ignores the very faint and short diagonal stroke of the second 'e' and then reads the two minims of the 'n' as a 'u'. I suspect that Tanner, writing in the eighteenth century, or his source, did exactly that, for Tanner refers to Nicholas as 'Nicolaus Linnensis (de Leuca)'.[3] Second, in the Bibliothèque Royale of Brussels, MS 4862/69, folio 41v, the name of Nicholas is spelled 'Nicholai de Linnea'. The word 'Linnea' consists of the initial 'L' followed by five minims and 'ea'. If again the 'e' is read as 'c' (not hard to do), and the line over the 'i' is ignored, the name might appear to be 'Lunica', a spelling which appears in Lynn Thorndike and Pearl Kibre's *Catalogue of Incipits of Medieval Scientific Writings in Latin*.[4] I think that both Tanner and Thorndike are mistaken when they put a [k] sound in Nicholas's name, and the error is compounded when the alleged sound is spelled with the letter 'k'. Since Peterhouse MS 75.9 was written before this history of error, I cannot agree that Dr Price's 'Leyk' is our Nicholas.

Nicholas does not say that he was associated with Oxford's Merton College, but I think it likely that he was. Merton, from the time of its founding in the thirteenth century, was a beehive of

[1] J. A. W. Bennett, *Chaucer at Oxford and at Cambridge* (Toronto, 1974), pp. 76–7.
[2] Derek J. Price, *The Equatorie of the Planetis* (Cambridge, 1955), pp. 47, 165–6.
[3] Tanner, loc. cit.
[4] Cambridge, Massachusetts, 1963, Section 652.

scientific inquiry.[1] By the fourteenth century Oxford led all universities in scientific achievement, and most of the astronomical studies took place at the Merton School of Astronomy. For instance, the Merton scholars copied the famed Alfonsine Tables, a collection of astronomical tables composed in the thirteenth century at Toledo. Naturally such tables had to be readjusted for the latitude and longitude of Oxford, and somebody had to figure what these were. Latitude was no problem. The latitude of any place is the altitude of the North Star and may easily be determined within a degree or so by the use of an astrolabe. Bishop William Rede (or Reed) of Merton College, who died in 1385, said that the latitude of Oxford was 51° 50',[2] a figure used by Nicholas of Lynn. Actually the latitude of Oxford is 51° 46', only 4' from Rede's figure. Longitude, which cannot be determined by simply taking a sight as latitude can be, was a different matter. Since no place was acknowledged to be 0° longitude, as Greenwich is now, any statement of longitude had to refer to two places. Thus if one wished to alter the Alfonsine Tables for Oxford, one had to know the longitudinal difference between Toledo and Oxford. An early scholar at the Merton School, according to Gunther, determined that Oxford was 16' east of Toledo.[3] Actually Oxford is 1° 16' west longitude or about 2° 44' east of Toledo. This discrepancy is responsible for some errors in Nicholas's eclipse tables. Such an error in computing longitude is not surprising when we recall that Spanish geographers, a little more than a century after the time of Nicholas, expected to find the coast of Asia about 70° west of Toledo. Nicholas never tells us that he belonged to the Merton School of Astronomy, but the conclusion seems inescapable that he was either a member of that school or a rare fourteenth-century Oxford astronomer who was not.

Apparently Nicholas spent his last days at or near Cambridge. He was ordained there as a subdeacon in 1410 and a deacon in

[1] Bennett, pp. 58–85, gives a superb description of the scientific activities at Merton College during the fourteenth century. See also Gunther, II, 42–65.

[2] Gunther, II, 56.

[3] Ibid., p. 45.

1411.[1] He is said to have died at Lynn and to have been buried there among the Carmelites.[2]

II

The one work which we have by Nicholas, except for a possible fragment of the *Inventio Fortunata*, is his Calendar, designed for the years 1387 through 1462. Nicholas, of course, was not the only calendar creator of his day. The calendar of Walter of Elvedene, whom Nicholas describes as a reverend teacher, was composed for the years 1330 through 1386.[3] In 1380, John Somer, also mentioned by Chaucer, wrote a calendar to run from 1387 through 1462, paralleling the dates of Nicholas's Calendar, and dedicated it to the Princess Joan, widow of the Black Prince and mother of King Richard II. Calendars in the fourteenth century were designed for multiples of 19 years, the approximate time the moon takes to return to whatever position it occupied when the cycle began. The initial year of such a cycle was called a golden year, as were the years 1330, when Walter of Elvedene began his calendar, and 1387, when Nicholas of Lynn and John Somer began theirs. This lunar period, called a decennovenal cycle by Nicholas, is called a Metonic cycle today.

Normally a medieval calendar gives various kinds of information: saints' days with their Sunday or dominical letters, sunrises and sunsets throughout the year, twilights, new and full moons, solar and lunar eclipses, some planetary information, dates of movable feasts, medical information (especially concerning proper times for phlebotomy or blood-letting), and astrological information pertaining to all of the above. The usual calendar is spiced with fascinating drawings: attractive blue and gold sketches of eclipses; a drawing of a man showing which signs of the zodiac relate to his various bodily parts; or once in a while a volvelle, which shows the phases of the moon by means of a circular piece

---

[1] A. B. Emden, *A Biographical Register of the University of Cambridge to 1500* (Cambridge, 1963), p. 370.

[2] Tanner, loc. cit.

[3] For more information concerning Walter of Elvedene see Emden, *A Biographical Register of the University of Cambridge to 1500*, pp. 210–11.

of perforated vellum pivoting over a page in the manner of our modern foreign language verb wheels. When calendars became obsolete, because the specific years for all the new and full moons, and of course eclipses, had passed, the folios were sometimes scraped clean and re-inked with the same information brought up to date. Parts of calendars on occasion developed an interest of their own and were copied separately. For instance, a portion of Nicholas's Calendar containing only medical information was copied for the use of physicians in 1470, eight years after the Calendar became obsolete. The language of the calendars was Latin, and usually they were written in what has come to be known in England as a university book hand, although calendars were copied in a variety of European handwritings well beyond the time of the introduction of printing.

No manuscript survives, so far as I know, containing the complete Calendar of Nicholas of Lynn, although several survive that are almost complete. Others have only part of the Calendar, some have been altered for Metonic cycles that occur after 1462, and a few have parts added from other calendars. The following description of Nicholas's Calendar is taken from the best of the manuscripts, all of which I shall discuss presently.

The first folio or first two pages of the Calendar contains a prologue. Nicholas says that he is a Carmelite friar at Oxford and that he dedicates the Calendar to John of Gaunt, whom, as we have seen, he calls not only Duke of Lancaster but also King of Castile and Leon. Since his marriage in 1372 to Constance of Castile, John of Gaunt had claimed the kingship of Castile, but his claim did not come to much until April 1386, when King Richard II of England placed a symbolic crown of Castile on John's head. John then led an unsuccessful expedition to conquer Castile; after the failure of this attempt, in September 1387, he renounced the kingship.[1] Accordingly, he was known as King of Castile for little more than the year which began in April 1386. Nicholas of Lynn wrote his Calendar in 1386 and called John, presumably in order to pay respect to the newly official title, King of Castile and

[1] *DNB*, XXIX, 421, 425.

Leon.[1] But only six manuscripts contain that title for John. The others, apparently, were copied after John renounced the Spanish crowns and may be assumed to be later and therefore more likely to attract scribal error.

After Nicholas identifies himself and John of Gaunt, he says that he is writing a Calendar to run for four decennovenal (Metonic) cycles, beginning in 1387. In the manner of astronomers, he says, he begins his day at noon on the previous day. The Calendar of John Somer did no such thing, and therefore Nicholas's dates are later than John's. Accordingly, information taken from Nicholas's Calendar is easy to identify. Nicholas says that he offers the following information for each day of the year: the extent of daylight hours with the twilights for the latitude of Oxford; new and full moons as they occur; time from midnight until sunrise, from sunset until midnight, from noon until sunset, and from sunrise until noon; the same times to and from the dark edge of twilight; the altitude of the sun with the length of the shadow of a six-foot man for every daylight clock hour of the year; the determination of the ascendants and the beginnings of the celestial houses for every day of the year; solar and lunar eclipses for the 76-year period with the times of their beginnings and endings, their durations, and their amplitudes, with tables and charts; and individual tables explaining the ascendants of celestial houses, the dignities and strengths of the planets, the placing of the planets in their zodiacal signs, the positions of the moon, movable feasts, and the continuation of the motion of the sun, that is, the perennial 'slippage' of the Julian calendar. At the end he promises a series of canons or rules which are to explain not only the entire Calendar but also medical practices at times shown by celestial configurations to be safe.

After this impressive prologue the actual month-to-month calendar begins with the month of January. Each month extends to one and a half or two folios, that is, three or four pages. The first page of each month shows the days of the month, dominical or Sunday letters, a Roman calendar, a saints' calendar, the place

---

[1] In the late fourteenth century the King of Castile was also the King of Leon.

of the sun on the ecliptic, and the times of sunrise, sunset, and the twilights. On the following pages appear the full and new moons during the four Metonic cycles; the various times from midnight or midday to dawn, sunrise, sunset, and the dark of night; and then for each daylight hour of the month the altitude of the sun and the length of the shadow of a six-foot man. This last is very important because it is unique among medieval calendars. Chaucer, as is explained below, uses this particular information in at least three places: the Introduction to the Man of Law's Tale, the Nun's Priest's Tale, and the Prologue to the Parson's Tale. After the shadow scale, Nicholas follows the same sequence for each of the eleven remaining months.

In most manuscripts the sequence of months is followed by solar and lunar eclipse tables and charts. Nicholas's knowledge of the eclipses is fairly good. He apparently calculated his eclipses from the Alfonsine Tables altered for the latitude and longitude of Oxford, as he knew them. Usually these alterations were accurate (I have compared them with a computerized list of fourteenth-century eclipses visible from Oxford[1]), but occasionally the good people at Merton, evidently forgetting that the world was not made of glass, began their visible eclipses before the rising of the eclipsed sun or moon or ended their visible eclipses after the eclipsed body had set. In general, Nicholas was accurate.

The eclipses are followed by a table of ascendants of houses for each degree of each sign of the zodiac, or, as we would have it, for each day of the year. Next is a table which tells what hour of the day or night a planet reigns. It is followed by a table for the computation of movable feats. On the next page are two tables. The first offers the motion of the sun, that is the amount of discrepancy between the position of the sun on a given day in 1385 and its position in subsequent years, the alteration being caused by the error of the Julian calendar. The second explains how to discover the dignities or influential positions of the planets in the signs of

[1] I am pleased to acknowledge the help of Dr Manfred Kudlek of the Institut für Informatik, Hamburg, who graciously furnished me with a computerized list of all solar and lunar eclipses, including every detail of each eclipse, which could have been seen from Oxford between the years 1308 and 2038.

the zodiac. The final table in the Calendar shows how to determine the zodiacal sign of the moon for each day. At the end of the Calendar are placed the canons or descriptive passages which explain all that preceded plus the rules for bleeding or administering medicine to a patient.

The first canon explains the various degrees of the zodiac given to the sun in the Calendar. Nicholas says that the figures in the Calendar are adjusted to the year 1385, a convenient year because it is one year after leap year and immediately precedes the year in which Nicholas was working. However, he tells the reader how to compute the true place of the sun for any year. The second canon discusses the lengths of the artificial and vulgar days and the twilights for the latitude of Oxford. The length of an artificial day was from sunrise until sunset, a vulgar day from the beginning of morning twilight until the end of evening twilight.[1] To Nicholas twilight meant about the same as our term 'astronomical twilight', that is the time when the sun is between 0° and 18° below the horizon. Nicholas's twilight was a little more than that, about − 20°. The third canon considers the new and full moons during the four Metonic cycles of the Calendar, and in the fourth canon Nicholas talks about the clock time of sunrise, sunset, and the beginnings and endings of twilights. In the fifth canon he turns to the clock hours during the artificial day. To Nicholas noon was always the time when the sun was at its zenith. The time from noon until noon was divided by 24, and each of those divisions was called an equal or clock hour. The unequal hours, on the other hand, were compounded by dividing the period from sunrise until sunset by twelve, just as they were in the Bible (Matthew 20: 1–16). In this section Nicholas explains the use of the tables to determine the time in clock hours and minutes by measuring the shadow of a six-foot man or any other object of similar height. In doing so he gives a tortured explanation of interpolation, which in the fourteenth century must have been in the springtime of development. In the sixth canon he analyses the unequal hours by means of a plumb line and more shadows, adding the calculations

---

[1] As Chaucer carefully explained to little Lewis: *Treatise on the Astrolabe*, II, Sections 7 and 9.

for leap year and each of the three succeeding years and explaining how the unequal hours vary if one strays to the north or south of Oxford. The seventh canon explains the tables of solar and lunar eclipses. The eighth canon is concerned with the times of ascendance of the great astrological houses. In the world of Nicholas, and that of today's astrologers too, the heavens surrounding the earth were divided into twelve segments, each extending from the north point of an observer's horizon to the south point. The terrestrial observer may see only six houses because the others are below the horizon. Each object in the sky passes through each of the twelve houses in a twenty-four hour period, and in each house each celestial object has a different effect on the welfare of man. The ninth canon tells which sign of the zodiac the moon is in at any time. This information was very important to medieval physicians, because, Nicholas tells us, if a patient were bled with the moon in an inauspicious sign, he might haemorrhage and die. The tenth canon is concerned with the computations of the movable feasts, namely Septuagesima Sunday, Easter, and Pentecost. The means of computation involves the dominical or Sunday letters, that is those letters of the alphabet from A through G assigned to the first seven days of the year and repeating throughout.[1] Nicholas, never dreaming that in time his Julian calendar would be replaced by the Gregorian calendar, tells how to compute the movable feasts for the next millennium.

In the eleventh canon Nicholas turns to the duties of a physician and explains the regulations for bleeding. Nicholas here says that he depends upon the *Centiloquium* of Ptolemy, as interpreted by one Haly, and on the works of Campanus. Claudius Ptolemy lived in the second century A.D. and wrote a book which we know as the *Centiloquium*. Haly may have been the tenth-century physician Haly Abbas, the eleventh-century Ali ben Ridhwan, who wrote a commentary on Galen, or the eleventh-century astrologer Ali ibn Abí Al-Rajjál.[2] Campanus may have been Campanus of

[1] When January 1 was a Sunday, the dominical letter was A; when January 1 was a Saturday, the letter was B; for Friday, a C, etc.

[2] For Haly Abbas see C. H. Talbot, *Medicine in Medieval England* (London, 1967), pp. 28–30. For the others see Walter Clyde Curry, *Chaucer and the Medieval Sciences* (New York, 1926), p. 245, n. 44. Chaucer mentions a Haly

Novara, who lived in Italy in the thirteenth century but who apparently said nothing that Nicholas says he did.[1] Blood-letting or phlebotomy was perhaps the principal cure for almost everything. According to Ptolemy and Haly as reported by Nicholas, blood-letting depends on the direction of flow of the humours, and that, like the tides of the sea, depends on the moon. During the first and third quarters of the moon, we learn, the humours flow from the interior of the body to the exterior. During the second and fourth quarters, of course, they flow back. When the humours are flowing to the exterior, blood-letting is rather risky, for the physician might start something he could not stop. But when the moon is safe and the humours are flowing back towards the centre, a little blood-letting hurts no one and probably does a lot of good. But also be aware, we are warned, that every part of the body is associated with one of the signs of the zodiac. And if you touch a given part of the body with iron, the moon being in the zodiacal sign of that part of the body, then you have real trouble, for the humours tend to rush to that part of the body which has the moon in its sign. So the tiniest prick of a knife, under such conditions, is likely to start a haemorrhage. Humours also flow towards an injury: Campanus is quoted as saying that if the skin receives a blow from a stick or a stone, and the skin is not broken, all the humours of the body will flow towards the injury, causing swelling and discoloration. But never casually bleed any part of the body without checking the moon. Campanus says that he saw a man with an injured arm. Gemini controls the arm, and that day the moon was in Gemini. The poor man, being ignorant in astronomy, bled himself in the arm and, although he had no sign of trouble aside from his injury, was dead within a week. Bleeding, obviously, was a very chancy thing.

In the twelfth canon Nicholas considers the giving and receiving of medicine, mainly laxatives. Today physicians do not hesitate to prescribe laxatives when needed. But when the medieval patient

[1] *Campanus of Novara and Medieval Planetary Theory*, ed. & tr., Francis S. Benjamin Jr. and G. J. Toomer (Madison, Wisconsin, 1971), pp. 23–4.

(*CT*, I, 431), whom Robinson, following Curry, discusses briefly, *Works*, p. 662.

needed a laxative, his physician had to weigh many other matters. First he must recall that within the body of man, in addition to the four humours, are four powers: attraction, retention, digestion, and expulsion. Each of these powers is closely related to the humours within the body and to all of the conditions outside the body, especially to signs of the zodiac. Depending on the time of the year, one of the powers would be strong. Further, any medicine, such as a laxative, will have a stronger effect when the ascendant is in the same sign as one of the four bodily powers. And the physician must not forget that the date of compounding the medicine should depend upon the zodiacal positions of heavenly bodies. There are, of course, dangers if precautions are not observed. Ptolemy says that no-one should give laxatives when the moon and Jupiter are together at the zenith. Haly explains that Jupiter is a friend to all nature and does not enjoy seeing the body purged. Therefore it is wiser to give a laxative when Jupiter is out of sight, that is below the horizon, and cannot be offended. If a medicine is given at the wrong time, the best that can be expected is that the patient will be nauseated and will vomit. The worst is that he will die. But should the doctor wish the patient to vomit, he must avoid giving an emetic when the moon is in Leo. If people vomit when the moon is in Leo, they will vomit blood. Nicholas concludes the medical canons, and the Calendar itself, with the rather sensible admonition that, no matter what the pattern of the heavenly bodies, some people, normally the lower classes, are going to be sick, while at the same time some of the higher estate will enjoy good health.

Apparently the medical canons by Nicholas were treasured apart from the rest of the Calendar. Four manuscripts contain only these canons or a part of them. Two of the four look as if they were written in a late fifteenth- or early sixteenth-century hand, and one is firmly dated 1470. One may guess from the evidence of the extant manuscripts that even after the Calendar was obsolete, the medical information remained valuable and in demand.[1]

Nicholas's Calendar survives in fifteen manuscripts of various

---

[1] For more about the medieval physician and his duties see Talbot, *Medicine in Medieval England*, especially Chapters x and xi.

quality. I have given each manuscript a sigil and have arranged them in descending order of importance to students of both Nicholas and Chaucer. The first four, MSS L, S¹, A¹, and possibly D, might have been seen by Chaucer. Internal evidence suggests that the others were copied after Chaucer's death in 1400. The last three, MSS M, S², and Gg, appear to have been copied after the 1462 expiration of the Calendar.

MS L, Oxford, Bodleian, Laud Miscellaneous 662, offers no evidence that it was copied in the fifteenth century. It is complete except for one missing folio which gives some eclipses on the recto and part of the table of the ascendants of houses on the verso.

MS S¹, British Museum, Sloane 1110, also offers no evidence of having been copied after Chaucer's death. Full moons in the fourth Metonic cycle (1443–1462) are not written in, although space for them is provided. The last folio is missing.

MS A¹, British Museum, Arundel 347, is probably from the fourteenth century. Most of the full and new moon tables have been scraped clean, but a few have been altered for the years 1463–1519, the three Metonic cycles immediately following the expiration of the Calendar.

MS D, Oxford, Bodleian, Digby 41, could be late fourteenth or early fifteenth century. The manuscript's first pages are missing: the Calendar begins in April. The full and new moon tables for 1387–1405 have been altered for 1520–1538, the fourth Metonic cycle after the expiration of the Calendar. Many figures and tables are missing, including the identical information missing from MS L. Apparently MS D was copied from MS L after MS L lost a folio and possibly after 1405; therefore Chaucer may not have seen it.

MS B, Brussels, Bibliothèque Royale 4862/69, appears to be a fifteenth-century manuscript because among the saints on the date March 27 appear the words 'Resureccio domini', signifying, presumably, that Easter was on March 27 during the year the Calendar was copied. The earliest year that Easter was March 27 after the composition of the Calendar was 1407, and Easter fell on that date also in 1418, 1429, 1440, and 1502. The year 1407 must stand as a definitive terminus a quo to this manuscript; Chaucer could not have used it. The manuscript is complete except for the prologue.[1]

MS So, Society of Antiquaries of London 8, includes only the prologue and the months through July. Like MS B, MS So has the words '*Resureccio domini*' for March 27, suggesting a *terminus a quo* of 1407, and Chaucer could not have seen it. The full and new moon tables are proper for Nicholas's four cycles. Where those manuscripts heretofore listed were meticulous, although not absolutely accurate, about the lengths of a shadow cast by a sun with an altitude of less than one degree, MS So gives inaccurate approximations often in round numbers. This manuscript and the others which give approximate shadow lengths are less accurate in many ways than the manuscripts which give meticulous shadow lengths. Therefore, I suggest that the approximations were the work of a later scribe and not of Nicholas of Lynn.

MS As[1], Oxford, Bodleian, Ashmole 5, seems to be early fifteenth century. It includes the inaccurate approximations for shadow lengths contained in MS So. One table and some canons are missing. It includes a chart from the calendar of John Somer.

MS R, Oxford, Bodleian, Rawlinson C 895, may be early fifteenth century. It includes the inaccurate approximations for shadow lengths. The full and new moon figures are scraped away and rewritten in another hand to cover the years 1482–1538. Some of the tables and canons are missing.

MS Ad, British Museum, Additional 15209, may be from the late fourteenth or early fifteenth century. John of Gaunt in the prologue is not mentioned as King of Castile and Leon. Inaccurate approximations are given for shadows cast by a low sun. One scribal error states that the length of the shadow of a six-foot man is eight instead of six feet when the sun is at 45°. In the Introduction to the Man of Law's Tale, as is explained below, Chaucer uses this information quite correctly, proving that whatever manuscript Chaucer used, it was not this one. Many figures, tables, and

[1] MS B, Brussels, Bibliothèque Royale, 4862/69, also contains a copy of Chaucer's *Treatise on the Astrolabe*, which was edited with a long informative introduction in 1940. For a brief discussion of the copy of Nicholas's Calendar in this manuscript, see P. Pintelon, *Chaucer's Treatise on the Astrolabe MS 4862–4869 of the Royal Library in Brussels* (Antwerp, 1940), pp. 38–9.

canons are missing, but many are added from the calendar of John Somer. Eclipse information from both Nicholas and John Somer is included.

MS A², British Museum, Arundel 207, seems to be from the fifteenth century. Lengths of shadows cast by a low sun are approximations. It has the errors of MS Ad and therefore could not have been used by Chaucer, but it has nothing added from the calendar of John Somer.

MS As², Oxford, Bodleian, Ashmole 370, has, as do MSS B and So, the words 'Resureccio domini' for March 27, proving the manuscript to be no earlier than 1407. It was probably copied even later: its earliest eclipse is 1424, and its lunar tables begin in 1425. Incorrect approximations are used for shadows cast by a low sun.

MS As³, Oxford, Bodleian, Ashmole 391, contains in just two columns some of the medical canons by Nicholas.

MS M, Munich, Bayerische Staatsbibliothek, Codex Latinus Monacensis 10661, is unique in that it contains the date 1470. The part by Nicholas of Lynn is only the last two canons, which contain medical information.

MS S², British Museum, Sloane 3285, appears to be in a fifteenth-century hand and contains by Nicholas only the next-to-last canon and part of the last canon.

MS Gg, Cambridge University Library Gg V 37, also in a likely fifteenth-century hand, contains one and a half folios by Nicholas, namely the same material that is in MS S².

MS L is probably the surviving manuscript of Nicholas's Calendar that is best, earliest, and most likely to have been seen by Chaucer. Accordingly, all of the following comments concerning Chaucer's use of Nicholas's Calendar are based on MS L.

III

We know that Chaucer used Nicholas's Calendar because he says he did. In the Prologue to *The Treatise on the Astrolabe* Chaucer says:

> The thirde partie shal contene diverse tables of longitudes and latitudes of sterres fixe for the Astrelabie, and tables of the declinacions of the sonne, and tables of longitudes of citees and

townes; and tables as well for the governaunce of a clokke, as
for to fynde the altitude meridian; and many anothir notable
conclusioun after the kalenders of the reverent clerkes, Frere J.
Somer and Frere N. Lenne. (77–86)

The 'Frere N. Lenne' is, of course, Nicholas of Lynn. But the
problems are that either Chaucer did not write the Third Part to
The Treatise on the Astrolabe or the Third Part did not survive, and
that the information which Chaucer said he would put into the
Third Part does not appear in Nicholas's Calendar. Nicholas has
neither stellar tables nor terrestrial longitudes, although he does
give some commonplace information about the sun, the clock,
and the meridian, items that were discussed by just about everyone
who wrote on astronomy. Nor is there any more evidence of the
use of Nicholas's Calendar in Chaucer's promise concerning the
missing Fourth Part of *The Treatise on the Astrolabe*, where
Chaucer says that he will offer a table of the motion of the moon,
a table not appearing in Nicholas's Calendar but common in other
medieval astronomical treatises. In his statement about the missing
Fifth Part, however, Chaucer does say:

> In which fifthe partie shalt thou fynden tables of equaciouns of
> houses after the latitude of Oxenforde; and tables of dignitees of
> planetes. . . . (103–106)

Nicholas does give tables of the equations of houses and the
dignities of planets. Apparently John Somer's calendar does not
have a table of the equations of houses, and although Somer
has a table of what hour a planet reigns, he does not have a
table devoted solely to the dignities of the planets in their signs.
The assumption must be that Chaucer planned to use Nicholas's
Calendar in the unwritten or lost Fifth Part. But an assumption
concerning a non-extant text is not enough: we must look elsewhere.

Chaucer did use Nicholas's Calendar, especially his unique
shadow scale, in at least three places in *The Canterbury Tales*.
Knowing Nicholas's Calendar, we may, I think, learn more about
what Chaucer intended. Also, as we shall see shortly, an awareness

of Nicholas's Calendar raises some new problems in our knowledge of Chaucer's intentions.

Early in *The Canterbury Tales*, in the Introduction to the Man of Law's Tale, the Host makes two observations concerning the time. First he says that the sun has risen one quarter of the artificial day plus half an hour plus a bit more. Then he notices that shadows are just as long as the objects which cause them, and since he knew that the date was April 18, he concludes that the time is 10.00 a.m.:

> Oure Hooste saugh wel that the brighte sonne
> The ark of his artificial day hath ronne
> The ferthe part, and half an houre and moore,
> And though he were nat depe ystert in loore,
> He wiste it was the eightetethe day
> Of Aprill, that is messager to May;
> And saugh wel that the shadwe of every tree
> Was as in lengthe the same quantitee
> That was the body erect that caused it.
> And therfore by the shadwe he took his wit
> That Phebus, which that shoon so clere and brighte,
> Degrees was fyve and fourty clombe on highte;
> And for that day, as in that latitude,
> It was ten of the clokke, he gan conclude . . . . (*CT*, II, 1–14)

The second observation is far more direct and therefore easier to handle. The Host knows that on April 18 shadows at 10.00 a.m. are just as long as the objects which cause them. The Host was right; his statement agrees with Nicholas's shadow scale.[1] I also know that the Host was right because on one April 27, our Gregorian equivalent to Chaucer's Julian April 18, standing in the rare sunshine of Chaucer's island and latitude, I too measured a shadow and discovered that at 10.00 a.m. it was just as long as the object which caused it. *Quod erat demonstrandum.*

But the first observation by the Host presents a problem.

---

[1] That is Nicholas says so in MSS L, S^1, A^1, D, B, So, As^1, R, and As^2. In MSS Ad and A^2, the length of the shadow of a six-foot man is given as eight feet, an impossibility with the sun at 45°. MSS A^3, S^2, Gg, and M do not have the shadow scale.

Robinson in his edition of Chaucer states that one fourth of the artificial day plus half an hour plus a bit more comes close to 10.00 a.m.[1] Robinson is depending on the nineteenth-century scholar, Andrew Edmund Brae, who, miscalculating the position of the sun after it had passed one quarter of the solar arc, says that the first observation comes out to 10.00 a.m. and scorns the eighteenth-century Tyrwhitt, who, with severe doubts, concluded that the Host's first observation was to a clock time a bit after 9.00 a.m. and not to 10.00 a.m. at all.[2] Tyrwhitt was right. According to Nicholas the sun rose on that day at 4.47 a.m. and set at 7.13 p.m. The artificial day, which as I have said, means the time from sunrise until sunset, was 14 hours and 26 minutes long. One fourth the artificial day was 3 hours and 36 minutes. Add that to 4.47, which was sunrise, and we have 8.23 a.m. Add half an hour to that and we have 8.53. Chaucer's words 'and more' would take us to 9.00 a.m. or a little after, unless by 'and more' Chaucer meant an unlikely hour and seven minutes. Even if we solve the problem the way Robinson or Brae did, or even work it out on an astrolabe, as I did and Chaucer could have, the time still comes to about 9.00 a.m., and the Host establishes the time to be both 9.00 and 10.00 a.m. in one statement. I present no solution to this sticky problem but offer this information so that one may raise a glass to Tyrwhitt, whose proper reservations were squelched far too soon.

In the Nun's Priest's Tale there is another use of Nicholas's shadow scale. On the morning of the day that the fox seizes Chauntecleer, May 3,[3] a singularly unlucky day when mentioned by Chaucer,[4] Chauntecleer promenades through his barnyard

[1] *Works*, p. 690. Robinson errs when he says that when the sun is 56° from the South point, the time is 9.20. Actually it is about an hour earlier.

[2] *A Treatise on the Astrolabe of Geoffrey Chaucer*, ed. Andrew Edmund Brae (London, 1870), pp. 68–71. Brae redefines the artificial day to suit his own conclusion.

[3] The date is May 3 because the sun is in the 21st degree of Taurus, which, according to Nicholas, is May 3. Professor Pratt emends 'Syn March bigan' on Line 3190 to 'Syn March was gon', making much more sense to the passage. See *The Tales of Canterbury*, ed. Robert A. Pratt (Boston, 1974), p. 244.

[4] Cf. *CT*, I, 1462–3, and *Troilus and Criseyde*, II, 56. The scribe of MS A² very cautiously labels May 3: 'Dies egritudinis'.

and tells from the sun's position that the time is prime or 9.00 a.m.:

Whan that the month in which the world bigan,
That highte March, whan God first maked man,
Was compleet, and passed were also,
Syn March bigan, thritty dayes and two,
Bifel that Chauntecleer in al his pryde,
His sevene wyves walkynge by his syde,
Caste up his eyen to the brighte sonne,
That in the signe of Taurus hadde yronne
Twenty degrees and oon, and somwhat moore,
And knew by kynde, and by noon oother loore,
That it was pryme, and crew with blisful stevene.
'The sonne', he seyde, 'is clomben up on hevene
Fourty degrees and oon, and more ywis'. (*CT*, VII, 3187–99)

Chauntecleer was quite correct. On May 3, according to Nicholas, the sun was at Taurus 21° 6'. At prime or 9.00 a.m. on that day the altitude of the sun was 41° 5' or Chauntecleer's 'Fourty degrees and oon, and more ywis'. If Chauntecleer had used a bit more of the knowledge that came to him 'by kynde', he would have known that if at that moment a six-foot man had appeared in the barnyard, his shadow would have been six feet ten inches long. Chaucer positively received this information from Nicholas of Lynn and not from John Somer. Nicholas, as I said above, began his astronomical day at noon on the previous day, but John Somer began his later: in John Somer's calendar May 3 is labelled as Taurus 22°.

At the beginning of the Prologue to the Parson's Tale Chaucer makes another observation concerning the time. He says that the sun was just less than 29° and sinking, that his shadow was about eleven feet, and that the time was 4.00 p.m.:

By that the Maunciple hadde his tale al ended,
The sonne fro the south lyne was descended
So lowe that he nas nat, to my sighte,
Degreës nyne and twenty as in highte.

Foure of the clokke it was tho, as I gesse,
For elevene foot, or litel moore or lesse,
My shadwe was at thilke tyme, as there,
Of swiche feet as my lengthe parted were
In sixe feet equal of proporcioun.
Therwith the moones exaltacioun,
I meene Libra, alwey gan ascende . . . (*CT*, X, 1–11)

This passage, which so obviously depends on Nicholas's shadow scale, swirls with difficulties. Most of these have been considered in the past. The first is that the Manciple begins his tale in the morning. Now it is 4.00 p.m. In many manuscripts, however, the time is given as 'ten of the clokke'. The modern emendation to 'foure of the clokke', in spite of the morning hour of the Manciple's Tale, seems justified. After all, the sun is not sinking at 10.00 in the morning and is not there at all at 10.00 p.m. In medieval handwritings a Roman 'ten' and an Arabic 'four' were similar: the Roman 'ten' was, and is, an 'X'; the Arabic 'four' was an 'X' closed by an arc over the top. Thus a 'four' with part of the ink rubbed away could easily be copied as a 'ten'. But much more convincing evidence comes from Nicholas. Had the time really been ten and the sun at the elevation stated, the date would have to be pushed back to March 2, and the final tale of the Canterbury Pilgrimage would have been told some six or seven weeks before the Pilgrims left Southwark.[1] The second problem is that Libra is not the moon's exaltation but Saturn's. Libra at 4.00 p.m. in mid-April was rising. Skeat, about a century ago, suggested that Chaucer made a mistake.[2] He probably did. Nicholas of Lynn in his table of the dignities of the planets in their signs makes it clear that the exaltation of Libra is Saturn. The third problem is one of dates. At 4.00 p.m., the passage tells us, the sun was less than 29° high. According to Nicholas, at 4.00 p.m. on April 17 the sun was

[1] For another opinion see Edward S. Cohen, 'The Sequence of *The Canterbury Tales*', *Chaucer Review*, IX (1974), 190–4. Mr Cohen suggests that Chaucer moved the Parson's Tale from 4.00 p.m. to 10.00 a.m. of the last day but neglected to remove the reference to the sinking sun.

[2] *A Treatise on The Astrolabe Addressed to His Son Lowys by Geoffrey Chaucer, A.D. 1391*, ed. W. W. Skeat, Chaucer Society Publications, No. 29 (London, 1872), p. lxiv.

at 28° 57', and on April 18 it was 29° 11'.[1] This means that the passage can apply only to April 17 or earlier. Robinson's suggestion of April 20[2] must be incorrect. Presumably we may read here that Libra was in its first few degrees of ascendency over the horizon. If the date was the latest possible, April 17, the sun according to Nicholas was in the fifth degree of Taurus, and Libra according to my own (and undoubtedly Chaucer's) astrolabe, was exactly 3° in ascension. All of these calculations fit properly for the Prologue to the Parson's Tale, but we now are led into the fourth and final problem: the date, April 17. How can we be at the end of the Canterbury Pilgrimage on April 17 when the Introduction to the Man of Law's Tale, which is traditionally placed early in the pilgrimage,[3] was dated April 18? J. D. North of Oxford, who considered this matter, concluded no more than that in Chaucer's mind the pilgrimage took place in April, as we learn from the first three words of *The Canterbury Tales*.[4] But Chaucer normally has a meaning assigned to each date and time. The 10.00 a.m. time on April 18 was used, one may guess, because, according to Nicholas, that is the only moment in the year when the sun is at 45° and the time of day is an hour unaccompanied by fractions of an hour or minutes. Now I wish to offer an unsubstantiated suggestion. Because every identifiable date in *The Canterbury Tales* takes place between January and July and between 1387 and 1394,[5]

[1] Nicholas's solar times are designed for the first year after leap year. For other years he offers two slight adjustments: one based on the differences among the first, second, and third year after leap year and leap year itself; the other based on the 'motus solis' or the yearly change in the Julian calendar. Both of the adjustments are so slight that Nicholas advises the user of the calendar to take little notice of them unless he is projecting many years to the future. There was no reason for Chaucer to avoid Nicholas's advice. Even with these adjustments, however, the latest date to fit the conditions here is April 17, except in the leap year itself, when it is April 16.

[2] *Works*, p. 765.

[3] Fragment II (B¹) of *CT* contains no reference that specifically places it before or after another fragment. It is found after the Cook's Tale in the manuscripts, and certainly no one has ever suggested that it could possibly follow the Introduction to the Parson's Tale.

[4] J. D. North, 'Kalenderes Enlumyned Ben They', *Review of English Studies*, New Series XX, No. 78 (1969), pp. 129–54; No. 79 (1969), pp. 257–83; No. 80 (1969), pp. 411–44. See especially No. 80, pp. 422–6.

[5] Ibid., passim.

it would seem that these dates, rather than presenting a chronological sequence for *The Canterbury Tales* and their links, are useful only for symbolic purposes. Thus the April 17 date following the April 18 date is not significant. But consider: the tone of the Parson's Tale is fitting for Good Friday. The joyous arrival in Canterbury would be fitting for Easter. In 1394 Good Friday was April 17.

In conclusion Chaucer did use the Calendar of Nicholas of Lynn, not in *The Treatise on the Astrolabe*, where he mentioned it, but in *The Canterbury Tales*. He did not, however, use it to give a final chronological organization to *The Canterbury Tales*. He used it instead as a source of information concerning specific hours and days which were necessary for his entire artistic scheme. That is, he was content to use Nicholas's Calendar as a time and date telling device, and after all, that is what a calendar is for.

II

Some Reflections on Critical Method

GEORGE KANE

SOME years ago[1] it struck me as an interesting project to compare the handling of their common central situation, the pursuit of a reluctant male by an ardent female, in the anonymous fourteenth-century romance *Sir Gawain and the Green Knight* and Shakespeare's *Venus and Adonis*; I fancied that I might learn something about the relation between tone and meaning from two excellent poets' handling of that rather special situation. I never got to make the comparison; to prepare myself for it I read the critical literature of the works, and the effect of doing so was to turn me from the poets to their critics, and to some elementary considerations of method. The respective disagreements between critics over these two poems proved to be extreme, and I could only wonder whether this was an inevitable situation.

I suppose my concern with method relates to my particular generation of university teachers of English, which has never been allowed to take the character of its occupation for granted. I entered the university near the end of an age of respect for authorities, great academics of the immediate past. My teachers, students of Kittredge, Klaeber and W. P. Ker, used to refer familiarly to those men, but their names never failed to induce awe in us. We saw ourselves as puny successors to a race of giants, and our first adjustment was to come to terms with our own insignificance. Then even before we had fully formed our attitudes to our profession it was subjected to various challenges: from Dr I. A. Richards, from Downing College and its magazine, and from the

[1] This essay derives from an inaugural lecture delivered at King's College London in 1967.

great American critics. Precipitated from hero-worship into reappraisal of our newly formed professional selves and their preconceptions we could take none of the approaches or methods that we had inherited for granted. In the new situation there was an absence of assurance, either from the support of authority or from a sense of knowledge of right procedures. And now in recent years, as if that were not enough, the changes in our own society and the world have given fresh point to a question which every professional student of literature must at some time have asked himself: wherein lies the validity of our occupation?

The old answer, that the value of our study lies in the training of minds and the increase of knowledge, cannot be immediately bettered. But it seems impossible not to wonder how well we serve that purpose in promoting or condoning the proliferation of discordant opinions, however ingeniously, learnedly, plausibly argued. Might not the disagreement be a symptom of deficiency in our methods? To be sure, the study of literature, because of its subject and the nature of its medium, is among the most difficult of all branches of learning. But is it really so difficult that it cannot be made more efficient? There should in principle, one presumes, be right and wrong ways of thinking about any given set of phenomena, even about a poem centuries old; and if that presumption is sound, then the right ways efficiently followed should lead to results not necessarily identical—since differences, merely, between the personalities of individual critics would rule that out —but necessarily congruent, differing only as various aspects of the same critical and interpretative truth.

How far the criticism of my two poems is from instancing such congruency I shall now show. My quotations throughout are direct and authentic, but I will not locate or identify them because no good purpose would be served by doing so; I have also refrained from using immediately recent material as possibly too fresh in people's minds.

I begin with *Sir Gawain and the Green Knight*. Here there is agreement in one particular at least, about the excellence of the poem. I read that 'it is one of the great poems of the Middle Ages in English, which is to suggest that it is greater than nearly all poems except a few by Shakespeare'. It is said to have 'an almost flawless structure'; 'it has superlative art in its fashioning; it is mature, deliberate, richly seasoned'; it exhibits 'sophisticated familiarity with varied aspects of aristocratic life and thinking'; 'a gracious comedy of manners is enacted' in it; it is 'one of the few undoubtedly aristocratic poems of the English Middle Ages extant'; 'even Chaucer's *Troilus* is less consistently courtly than *Sir Gawain and the Green Knight*'. There has been corresponding speculation about its author: whether the poem's 'exquisite deftness of touch and the over-all polish' must not mean that he was 'a courtier, a man of leisure and learning, at ease among people of refined tastes', possessing 'the intimate awareness of one who had been born to high estate and "gentilesse"'. In any event, says a modern book, 'certainly in tone *Sir Gawain* is the most continental of English romances'; 'the urbanity of the poem . . . looks forward to the courts of the Medicis and Elizabeth'; the highest possible praise, it appears.

No doubt everyone I have just quoted would instantly agree on the need for judicious praise in literary criticism, that praise should be not excessive but appropriate, and conferred for appropriate reasons. But not all can have observed that need, for with agreement about the excellence of the poem the consensus ends; the rarity of further agreement implies that in some cases at least the poem was admired for the wrong, for inappropriate reasons. The high praise plainly registers the affective capability of the poem, but that same capability may have impeded its understanding and assessment. Anyone who openly argued that a poem which engages him powerfully must be correspondingly excellent in all respects, or that those elements of a poem which engage him most powerfully are necessarily its most significant elements, would be smiled at. As soon as we express such propositions nakedly their fallaciousness is evident. But how often are they expressed? How often do they operate, unexpressed and subconsciously, to cloud critical judgement?

Very often, I suspect, in the case of *Sir Gawain*. We call the

poem a romance. For a start the various, more specific character-
izations applied to it have been such as to put that very broad and
barely classificatory label to severe strain. At one extreme it has
seemed merely entertainment, a form of 'play' in the sociological
sense; at the other a deeply symbolical spiritual document. We
can disregard the former description as not literary; the latter
would at least historically be a genuine possibility. The variety of
views between is considerable. For instance I read that 'the primary
purpose of the poet is to show what a splendid man Gawain was,
. . . what a perfect knight can do when he is forced to face the
unknown', but otherwise that 'the focus of the story is on the
extension and consequences of [Gawain's] blunder, which is misuse of heroic, or courtly ritual'; and that the poet 'utilises a
magnifying lens to throw into sharp focus the assumptions of
romance, revealing . . . the weaknesses as well as the strengths of
the knightly code'. A qualification of the second view runs to the
effect that 'the subject of this romance is romance itself', that the
poem expresses 'an ambivalent attitude to the romance ideal', the
limitations of which 'were a particular fourteenth-century concern', and that the poem is actually 'a gently satiric anti-romance'.
I also find references to its 'high comedy', to its 'quintessentially
human' or 'rich but delicate comedy', to the 'spirit of comedy' in
which its central action develops. It is 'essentially a comic poem',
even though 'from the standpoint of romance' it 'has been a
tragedy'. The poem, this characterization goes on, 'is thus both a
tragic romance . . . and an unromantic comedy'. This view is
rhetorically impressive, but elsewhere I find a contrary view, that
the romance contains 'not the slightest questioning or probing of
the social values of the aristocratic caste'.

This last opinion is not, however, widespread. The majority of
interpretations assume that the principal and most significant
motive of the romance is some kind of demonstration, of which
the central agency is the testing of Gawain, especially in the three
successive assaults the Lady makes on his 'virtue'. But there is no
general agreement about the subject of the demonstration, about
what precise quality in him is being tested. In one view, confi-
dently expressed, the temptations are simply an exemplum of

admirable behaviour: 'Gawain resisted the Lady because he was the man he was, one deeply committed to the ideal of chastity'. In another, asserted with equal confidence, the subject of the test is Gawain's 'loyalty to his host', the Lady's husband. The virtues specifically at stake are his 'courage, honour, loyalty and courtesy'. This second view is supported by an ingenious adjustment of moral values: 'The term *synne* is used [in the text] with reference to unchastity, but according to the logic of Gawain's thought we see it to be in effect a venial sin, more important for its implications of secular failure than in itself . . . the betrayal of [the husband] . . . is . . . the truly heinous offence to be avoided'. The critic who found the poem both a 'tragic romance' and an 'unromantic comedy' senses no problem of selection: the Lady's temptations test Gawain in many respects, 'not only continence and a bargain with the host but courtesy, loyalty and the dangers of sin'. The temptations have also been read as social and literary criticism. Because they reverse the male and female sex roles they have been held to stand what is called the courtly love convention on its head and thus to imply 'satire of the deification of women'; 'these scenes are high-style parody of a discredited literary convention' or (in the same essay) 'gentle mockery of manners mistaken for morals'.

There is a corresponding variety of opinions about the meaning of the romance. It will be recalled that one reader thought it merely playful entertainment. Another finds in it a remarkably general moral, that 'if we wish to act to our highest capacity we must be loyal to those who deserve our loyalty. In a word we must be obedient to our station and our social duty'. Yet another discerns a more specific intention in the poet, to contrast the 'incipient corruption' of 'Arthur's young court' 'in matters of sex and loyalty' with the 'morally superior' court of Bercilak. Recalling that it is the latter's wife who conducts the temptation we may think that reading poorly supported by the actual text. There is one even more remote: the temptation of Gawain proceeds according to the specified stages of hamartiology, as 'widely applied to the legends of the Saints', and is 'congruent with the patristic tradition'; the romance is deeply symbolical of spiritual truths, a 'drama of the human soul' on its journey through life, in which the two ladies in the castle 'represent the two personified aspects of the Christian Fortuna'; they and the Lord of Hautdesert are 'agents of Divine Providence'.

One response to the situation I have sketched is to interpret it as an invitation to syncretism. This I find in an appraisal of the poem which describes it as 'reflecting a many faceted solidity which is both comic and serious. It is meant to entertain and to some extent teach a sophisticated audience. It is a combination of secularism and religion, of the marvellous and the real, of the subjective and the objective, of the decorative and the direct, of the vague and the clear, of courtesy and horror, of the elevated and the plain.' By admitting so many possibilities of categorization that description certainly registers the difficulty of the work. Another response, to assert stoutly that 'There is nothing problematical in the poem', may seem self-delusive. A third, my own, is purely one of dismay at such lack of agreement.

Lest this situation should be thought peculiar to medieval studies, I quickly turn to *Venus and Adonis*, about which there is also some diversity of critical opinion. Shakespeare criticism, however, scores one point: some of its exponents have been bold enough to allow that this might be an unsuccessful poem. As long ago as 1817 it was called 'hard, glittering and cold'; later in that century it was judged 'a model of what a young man of genius should not write on such a subject'. In our time it has been found 'uninspired and pitilessly prolix', 'destitute of feeling for the human situation', 'a manufactured poem, consistently constructed for the market'. 'Desperate, indeed, is the word for *Venus and Adonis* as a whole . . . there is strain, there is conceit, there is bad taste.' 'Shakespeare falls between the serious and the comic.' The poem 'shifts disconcertingly from frigid conceits to moving pathos'. 'This wavering is symptomatic of [the author's] lack of perfect control.' The poem is 'an exercise in versifying'. Against these views are set clean contrary ones. It has been called 'the first rank product of a mind which for the variety and excellence of its fruits has never been surpassed'. It has seemed 'a great work of release, an assertion of natural energies', or 'the paean of the young poet, singing the song, not of Ovid, but of his native countryside, a song of earth, the song of a new nation . . ., the song of youth'. It has (somewhat inconsistently) been said to be 'a complete artistic success, despite some flaws or weaker passages . . . . all things work together'. The same critic writes of 'the imaginative unity of the poem . . . in its view of elemental and human passions as a feast for the mind and spirit: as sometimes moving and sometimes amusing, but always offering an absorbing living spectacle'. How splendid that sounds—until one tries to conceive the precise nature of such 'imaginative unity' and sees the description as a denial of formal significance to the poem.

Critics have had difficulty in identifying its effect. It has been called 'a kind of verbal painting', and less imprecisely, 'a series of beautiful and voluptuous pictures'. It has been characterized as both a 'verse romance', and an account of Adonis's revenge on Venus for her destruction of his mother Myrrha. Various critics have found in certain tonal elements of the poem effects other than of gravity; these they have variously identified. For one 'the rhetorical burlesque and the comic characterization of the legendary lovers travesty Neoplatonic notions of love'; the words and actions of Venus 'burlesque Renaissance styles' and 'romantic literary conventions'. For another there is 'obvious farce inherent in the representation of the Goddess of Love's failing to arouse passion in a mortal youth'. Shakespeare's intention (the term is used without evident unease) was 'to write a sensuous, sophisticated farce'. No matter with respect to accurate use of critical terms that Adonis is killed; our little farce is rounded with a death. For a third critic, indeed, the poem contains 'the spirit of . . . a romantic, that is to say a Shakespearean comedy'. A fourth calls it 'a sparkling and sophisticated comedy'; even 'the verse itself is comic'. Someone else writes of the poet's 'almost satiric' outlook, and finds his use of hyperbole 'ironic'; and still another sees the poem as 'the expression of the most savage irony known to him in literature'. Predictably the poem also acquires the label, 'wry, ironic comedy'. Still, the death of Adonis is troublesome. For the proponent of the 'verse romance' notion it is 'a result of inherent antipathies in nature'. For the discoverer of the 'spirit of comedy'

in the poem the metamorphosis of Adonis serves to put off grief,
to make 'the story light as a bubble and keep it floating'. For the
reader who found the poem 'sparkling' and 'sophisticated' the
grief of Venus is distanced 'by making her speeches burlesques of
conventional sixteenth-century Elizabethan complaints'. It comes
as no surprise then to find the poem called 'a tragicomedy of love'.
But against these views is the stern pronouncement that the
'dominant impression of *Venus and Adonis* is not really of a
"jocosity"'. Someone has actually called it 'essentially a tragic
poem'. To round off these differences there is an ingenious interpretation which identifies in the changing state of mind of Venus
'an Aristotelian anagnorisis'.

A corrective voice reminds us that the poem is 'not a comedy or
a tragedy. It is not a drama' but the narration of a myth; it
'interprets life through a fictional paradigm'. The author of that
cautionary view does not specify what aspects of life the paradigm
interprets, but such information is forthcoming from other
sources. One pronounces the poem as 'didactic a piece of work as
Shakespeare ever wrote' and reads it as an allegory of the destructive agency of 'sensual love', naturally symbolized in Venus, while
Adonis (the unloving) is 'reason in love, all truth, all good'. For
another interpreter the poem, somewhat vaguely, 'allegorizes the
generative impulse in its proper and improper force'; for another
it is 'a metaphysical commentary on the destruction of good by
evil'; for a third the boar which kills Adonis is 'death, the eternal
hunter'.

There is still more. *Venus and Adonis* has been described as a
'wholly impersonal' work. It is, however, also searched for auto-
biography. Its 'confused emotional quality' may relate to the
poet's 'revulsion from the physical fact of sex'. Elsewhere I read
that Adonis stands for the young man of the first fourteen sonnets;
his similar reluctance to propagate, 'and the close parallels . . . in
respect of imagery and theme make it certain that the connexion
exists'. Or the poem is the work of a commercial dramatist intent
on proving himself a sophisticated gentleman; it makes 'a claim to
social dignity for its author'.

Is it presumptuous to see the critical situation of these two poems as evidence of the inefficiency of a procedure of trial and error, assertion and counter-assertion (with occasional compromise) and no better assurance of correctness than the absence of contradiction? I do not know whether these situations are typical. The poems are peculiarly difficult, and such conflict of opinions as they have generated may not represent the best products of the professional or expert study of English literature. Even so, is it either inevitable or appropriate that the study of any literary topic, however difficult, should result in such chaos?

The answer ought to be that it is not. Obviously literary study can never develop an exact science: the affective element in our apprehension of literature excludes that possibility at the outset. The peculiar sensibility which initially drew most of us to our preoccupation is not subject to measurement, and its operation, indispensable to all kinds of literary study, can be tested for accuracy only by individual reenactment of the experience of a literary work. But as I understand literary criticism the operation of that sensibility is only one element of the critical process, namely a source of its data. A second, which subjects those data to description, analysis and explanation, is properly a reasonable, an intellective activity. Even if literary criticism were no more than the rationalization of subjective responses, it is manifest that such rationalization could be more or less skilful, more or less rational. It does not follow from the presence of a subjective element in a mental activity that subjectivity should there have free rein; if anything the contrary implication has force: such a situation calls for intellectual regulation of the subjectivity.

The beginning of such discipline in our study would be avoidance of certain solecisms of critical logic. When a critic of *Venus and Adonis* writes of the poem that 'we are struck by a certain note of cold sensuality which not all of Shakespeare's artistry can efface' his use of the term 'efface' makes critical nonsense out of what might be a valid insight. When a discussion of the same poem asserts, after maintaining its lack of unity of effect, that nevertheless 'Shakespeare was wholly successful in what he set out to do' the implicit *petitio principii* vitiates the exposition: the possibility of a truth of literary history that underlies the situation being identified is reduced. Critical perception is dimmed by a fog of fallacious argument, of unauthorized inference, of unsystematic synthesis. Yet even for us students of literature it should be possible to maintain distinctions between an assumption, a proposition and a hypothesis in the development of a discussion, or to understand what is meant by implication or by absolute proof, and what is involved in an assessment of probabilities.

Another possible control of subjectivity would be regulation of the use of evidence. There can, for instance, be no justification for critical assertions made in defiance of the text they relate to, but they are not uncommon, and they lead to misinterpretation. There is nothing in the actual text of *Sir Gawain and the Green Knight* to suggest the 'incipient corruption' of 'Arthur's young court'; indeed the poet expressly sets the action in the first, the golden age of Arthur's court. So one argument about the meaning of the poem is imperfectly founded. Someone tells us that 'Read as a chastity test the temptation makes Gawain practically a subject for canonization', whereas the poet states that Gawain was in great danger of succumbing, and was saved only by the grace of the Virgin Mary, patroness of chastity. So an argument about the subject of the testing, and thus of the poem, is poorly based. We read that Adonis was killed 'through the motiveless malignity of the wild boar'; the beast's *méchantise*, however, consisted in defending himself against a hunter and his pack of hounds. So an alleged similarity between Shakespeare's poem and *Hero and Leander* is reduced. Or we read that 'with the death of Adonis lust triumphed', in disregard of the thirty-line-long curse upon love which Venus pronounces beside his corpse.

Such practices I call critical solecisms. Another kind, at least as grave, is disregard of significant external information. Here is an instance. Part of the argument advanced for *Venus and Adonis* being a comedy is that 'the verse itself is comic'. Four lines in particular are singled out: these, we read, are 'so banal ... that one must explain their flatness as the result of either ineptitude or of dramatic propriety'. Their banality, supposing it to be genuine, was quite missed by a contemporary poet who was evidently impressed by the passage where they stand, for he made their content the subject of a substantial poem (not comical) and even echoed them in its title. That fact questions, to say the least, the modern critical response. Disregard of external information can lead to the basing of arguments on erroneous historical and critical generalizations. This occurs in the case for the comic or anti-romance quality of *Sir Gawain*. Its proponent, correctly observing that Gawain's crestfallen return to Camelot is likely to provoke a smile at his expense, then generalizes that 'comedy is not the stuff of which romance heroes are made'. Apart from Gawain's not being actually 'made' of comedy, he has forgotten the 'comedy' in the careers of beloved romance heroes like Horn and Havelok and William of Palerne and Perceval, and Bevis whose mother checks him by seizing hold of his ear (to name instances only from Middle English). Gentle ridicule of the hero can be a part of the effect of romances; the case thus lacks foundation. To turn back to *Venus and Adonis*, a part of the argument for its being a comedy has been that 'the tradition that Shakespeare followed was demonstrably comic'. But as far as I can ascertain *Venus and Adonis* was only the third English poem of its kind; of its two predecessors one only might possibly be called 'comic'; even that ends with a drowning and a suicide. The argument from tradition is thus not very strong. Much solecistic generalization has to do with the term 'Ovidian'; one cynically wonders how many of its users have read Ovid even in translation; certainly not the one who writes of the goddess and the boy that 'the events in the poem retell their Ovidian romance'. Such patent factual and critical inaccuracy is probably less misleading than the more insidious historical inaccuracy resulting from derivative generalizations. I have in mind the use by some critics of the term 'Ovidian' as if it explained everything about *Venus and Adonis*. Unless they mean by it no more than 'erotic' it explains nothing for me: the effects of the poem are remote from any that I can sense, or find identified by classical scholars, in *Metamorphoses*.

Another possible control of subjectivity would be a more disciplined use of critical terms. If I understand correctly, the terminology of criticism is the instrument of contact between its affective and intellective elements: identifying the subjective response by naming it contributes one set of the matrixes indispensable to the rational understanding and logical explanation of the phenomenon which is the poem. Therefore precision of identification of affects, that is the precise use of critical terms, and correctness of interpretation must be directly related. Moreover, such precision can itself operate as an intellectual control since it implies discrimination by comparison and should thus direct critical thinking to the logical relation of notions. By contrast the wider the application of a term of description or classification, the less its descriptive or classificatory value must become. Thus it is relatively uninformative to describe the absence of solemnity as comedy, or to identify a pathetic with a tragic effect. But still worse, the inappropriate use of such terms has a kind of stultifying absoluteness whereby that which is not tragic must be comic, and so on. A spurious logic of criticism is set up in which there is no middle term, no range of subtly differentiated effects between those extremely differentiated kinds. Sometimes the particular consequence is absurdity, as in the portentous assertion that the death and metamorphosis of Adonis were 'not intended to arouse tragic emotion', or in the waggish comment about the close of *Sir Gawain* that 'from the standpoint of romance the poem has been a tragedy', where the intended meaning must have been 'disaster'. In general however the slovenly use of critical terms produces simply dull confusion: identical responses by various critics imprecisely named appear to be conflicting; disagreement is multiplied, and the growth of understanding retarded.

Good logic, scholarly accuracy, and the precise use of critical language would improve situations like those just above. But the ultimate control of subjectivity must be through maintenance of a critical point of view, that is through consistently thinking about a poem in terms of its mode of existence. Some gross failures to do this will show what I mean. Someone calls the Lady of Hautdesert 'an honest English rose'; someone with apparent solemnity writes that Gawain's having fended off her sexual advances is 'To ... the glory of British literature'; someone apparently not familiar with the English observes that 'the icy, petulant Adonis is an English gentleman'; someone describes Venus as 'a forty-year old count-ess'. Such unilluminating nonsense could not be seriously written by anyone who kept in mind that a personage in a literary fiction exists only as an experience in the reader's imagination.

The critical point of view implies several presumptions of special relevance to our two poems: that a poem has by logical definition a normative meaning; that a successful poem functions by the interaction of all its parts; and that the whole significance of the unity of a poem, its 'meaning', is a product of relation between the inherent possible significance of what is represented and the quality of feeling generated by the mode of representation in the most general sense. In terms of such presumptions no inter-pretation of either poem ought to be acceptable which leaves any part of it out of account. But in the case of both our poems a main difficulty for critics has been the satisfactory correlation of all their respective parts.

The central problem seems to be one of tone. Both poets have elected to represent an essentially ludicrous situation. Cardinal elements in the action of *Sir Gawain*, and the whole action of Shakespeare's poem, are of a kind to have inherent significances, an *a priori* value, and to set up particular expectations of treatment. The question is how each poet valued the action in question, what meanings and feelings he sensed in it. These are essential parts of the whole meaning of the works and will reveal themselves principally in the tone of their representation, from which the attitudes of the poet to his subject and his audience might be inferred.

The critical disagreements, and the frequency of the term 'ambivalence' in discussion of both poems, point to the difficulty of each. But here too there is an elementary logic. For genuine ambivalence in a poem is either deliberate, in which event it is a function of the meaning of the poem, or unintentional, in which event it may well register fluctuation or imperfect realization of the poet's response to his subject, with whatever implications.

Critics of *Venus and Adonis* have at least recognized that their problem is one of tone: the necessary deliberateness of Shakes-peare's conflation of two fables from *Metamorphoses*, which radically changes the relation of his two personages, directs attention to his attitude to the action. They have identified tonal discords; the difficulty has been to account for them, for example to discover a significant relation between general elevation of the narrative through stylistic elaboration and occasional naturalism of an extreme character. Essentially laughable incident is reported in richly beautified language, with punctuations of grotesquerie. What the critics have not squarely faced is a choice of obligations: to reconcile all parts, to relate the various mixtures of effect, or to accept the implications of that being impossible about the poet and the poem.

In the case of *Sir Gawain* it may be that tones have simply been mis-heard, and the poem misread in consequence. The complexity here results from the poet's predicament as a narrator in representing Gawain's temptation. This must appear not merely genuine but extreme. The Lady's advances must seem irresistible and Gawain must nevertheless resist them; moreover, in his character as the knight of courtesy *par excellence* he must resist with grace: he cannot reject his temptress brutally or sharply. No doubt that combination of requirements taxed the poet. A second complicating circumstance derives from the alliterative tradition in which the poet worked. This afforded him an exceptional resource of vocabulary, to be sure, but its terms had been developed for derring-do, not for his delicate, even awkward amatory topic. And Gawain's accumulated reputation as an amorist will not have helped; the poet had to insist on his chastity if there was to be any element of doubt over the outcome of the temptation. Such insistence would be bound to affect his tone.

Critics in general hold the poet to have acquitted himself well: the temptation scenes, they write, exemplify lightness, subtlety and social poise; they are conducted with 'exuberant humour' in a 'romping style'; the talk between Gawain and the Lady is 'gay . . . banter'; the poet is 'as sophisticated as the cosmopolitan Chaucer'.

But even cursory comparison with the most nearly similar situations in Chaucer's poetry casts doubt on such opinions and sends one back to the text of *Gawain*; a realistic examination of the

Lady's manner of proceeding, which seems not calculated to succeed, makes to seem dubious the 'sophistication' of the temptation scenes (which, one then recalls, have been read as a satire of traditional attitudes to love). Her unmistakable offers of herself make the game too easy; her mention of her husband will put off Gawain by bringing the moral notion 'adultery' into his mind; telling him she is helplessly infatuated with him will more likely make him shy away from emotional responsibility than undertake it; she even tries to constrain him, and reproaches him for being a backward lover. One can see why an Edwardian critic gallantly excused her for her failure as 'inexperienced'.

Indeed the inexperience, when one compares the management of these scenes with Chaucer's representation of, for instance, the seduction of Criseyde by Diomede, might seem to be the poet's. The difference of psychological realism between them is of the same kind, if not of the same degree, as that between Mr B.'s attempts on Pamela's virtue and the seductions in *Les Liaisons Dangereuses*.

There is a further element of difficulty in the temptation scenes of *Sir Gawain*: the pietistic and moral expressions. Delighted to have Gawain prisoner at her mercy in his bed the Lady praises the Heavenly Lord for her good fortune; she begs God to reward Gawain for his small kindness in kissing and talking to her; when she leaves him for the time being with a loving kiss the two commend each other to Christ. In the second episode the poet plainly states that the Lady's temptations were designed to persuade Gawain to wrongdoing; Gawain, in the third episode, is described as anxious lest he should commit sin. These are strange words and notions to find in a 'courtly', 'sophisticated', 'aristocratic' poem; taken together with Gawain's angry self-justification at the end of the second beheading scene, a stock antifeminist topos echoing Jerome against Jovinian, they might rather suggest a clerkly, moralistic attitude. And that suggestion could redirect the interpretation of the romance. It might turn out that the social gloss of the poem is not so knowledgeably applied as has been argued. If so we should be the better critics for giving the poem appropriate praise.

It is of course easy to write destructive criticism as I have been doing. But there is a kind of criticism which both destroys and is constructive, namely self-criticism, and my task would have been harder or even needless if some of the writers from whom I have quoted had exercised this. Their sensibility and in some cases their learning are impressive. But their affirmations, denials and counter-affirmations can set up a confusion which, rather than stimulating the young judgement, may create a false impression of the supremacy of the affective element in literary study. I would rather see sensibility, the capacity for strong response, taken for granted and the intellectual element in criticism fostered. Not very long ago an educational bigwig was quoted in the press as proclaiming that our students nowadays are too sophisticated to be taken by the hand and shown the 'beauties' of literature. Perhaps so, perhaps not. But in any event they need more than ever to be taught to think acutely and reasonably about it, even if only so that they may become proficient in thinking acutely and reasonably about other matters. It might seem our business as teachers and critics both, to learn this ourselves so that we may show them the way.

III

Chaucer's Idea of an Idea

DONALD R. HOWARD

EVERY literary work was once an idea in its author's mind: when we read the work we grasp the idea at least in part, and whatever formal qualities we find in the work—unity or form or structure—could not exist without that idea. If we can suppose this, what can we suppose about the idea of *The Canterbury Tales*? Until recently most critics have supposed that Chaucer's idea of *The Canterbury Tales* was a simple one: they have said that the work is at base a realistic description of a four-day journey to Canterbury, that if the author had lived longer he would have added more tales, described overnight stops and the journey home, that the heart or backbone of the work is the tales themselves (especially the bawdy ones), and that in these his great achievement was in breaking with convention and going direct to life. In reaction to this estimate of *The Canterbury Tales* a more recent trend in Chaucer criticism has advanced an even simpler idea: that the pilgrimage to Canterbury is a metaphor for the pilgrimage of human life, that the pilgrimage as a penitential act is the heart or backbone of the work (or the 'fruit'), and that the tales are there-fore 'chaff'—which, however, I am happy to add, no amount of wind has managed to blow away.

All these opinions assume that *The Canterbury Tales* has a single controlling idea behind it, one that we can articulate and see executed in the work. If we politely suppose that each is correct (as Egeus would say) 'in some degree', then taken together they are 'the' idea of *The Canterbury Tales*. And this means that the idea is not a simple one at all but ornate, many-faceted, labyrinthine—may I say Gothic—in its complexity. Nevertheless, it is *an* idea which existed in *a* poet's mind and is embodied in *a* work. It is composed of many characteristic ideas of his period; but taken together it is singular, unique—may I say Chaucerian—in its individual embodiment.

This is the claim I made in my book *The Idea of the Canterbury Tales*;[1] if in this essay I repeat my claim in a mercifully shorter space I hope the repetition will verge toward clarity and refinement. I have claimed to have seen inside the mind of Geoffrey Chaucer and to have described the idea which existed in his mind, which moved him to write *The Canterbury Tales*, which informed its whole and its parts, which is embodied in it and makes it live— an outrageous claim, the daughter of Megalomania and Obsession, as it must seem—but I insist that it is less outrageous than previous claims. When a critic says that Chaucer meant to write over a hundred tales which he never wrote (because one ebullient character proposes that the others tell that many tales), or when a critic says that Chaucer meant to describe a journey home which he never described, in a kind of description no medieval author had written, they have made claims far more outrageous. They have claimed to know a startling, original plan which he had in mind but failed to accomplish. I claim to observe a plan sufficiently characteristic of his age which he had in mind and largely did accomplish.

To my claim there is still an objection which can be raised. The objector might say, 'You are presupposing an idea which existed in the author's mind and informs his work, but isn't this *idea* of an idea a modern one, the sort of conception Coleridge advanced when he spoke of "organic unity", the sort of superstition we hold when we praise a modern book for "tightness" or demote it for "sprawl" or "self-indulgence"?' But my reply is no. The kind of idea I have in mind is a medieval conception, one which was part of medieval aesthetics and rhetoric. It is what Erwin Panofsky[2] called 'the artist's quasi-idea'—a concept not of a transcendent realm like the Platonic ideas, nor yet only of remembered experience, but of a mental image in the artist's mind comparable to, but not the same as nor fully sharing in, the ideas which exist in the

[1] University of California Press, 1975.

[2] *Idea: A Conception in Art Theory*, trans. Joseph J. S. Peake (rpt. Icon Editions, 1968), esp. chap. 3.

mind of God. Panofsky showed how the Middle Ages, though it adopted on the whole a mimetic theory of art, held that the object of that mimesis was not 'nature' but the interior reality which exists in the artist's mind. The painter does not paint a rose; he paints his idea of the rose, and this idea or 'quasi-idea' is of a higher order than any single physical specimen and anterior to any artistic embodiment. Edgar De Bruyne in *The Esthetics of the Middle Ages*[1] describes the doctrine when he writes, 'The material work of art is not necessarily a faithful copy of the visible form (a roof is not a reproduction of a mountain range), but it is inevitably a representation of what the artist conceives in his soul. The form is above all an imitation of this spiritual model'. Dante in *De monarchia* II, 2, refers to the doctrine in what Panofsky calls a lapidary sentence: 'Art is found on three levels: in the mind of the artist, in the tool, and in the material that receives its form from art.'

Such an idea of an idea was present in the rhetorical writings of the Middle Ages and was thus part of the medieval conception of poetical composition. The emphasis was on the experience of the writer rather than of the reader, on the *making* of the poetical work. The best-known expression of the idea is in the opening lines of Geoffrey of Vinsauf's *Poetria Nova*: 'If a man has a house to build, his impetuous hand does not rush into action. The measuring line of his mind first lays out the work, and he mentally outlines the successive steps in a definite order. The mind's hand shapes the entire house before the body's hand builds it. Its mode of being is archetypal before it is actual.'[2] We know Chaucer was familiar with this passage because he translated it in the *Troilus*, assigning it to Pandarus as a thought which occurs to him as he plans to arrange the love affair.

About this medieval conception of a poetical idea there is a question which I side-stepped in *The Idea of the Canterbury Tales* and would like to consider in what follows. If we can fairly assume that Chaucer's idea of a poem squared with the medieval conception, did his understanding of that conception, his personal

[1] trans. Eileen B. Hennessy (New York, 1969), p. 142.
[2] trans. Margaret F. Nims (Toronto, 1967), pp. 16–17.

grasp of it and his private thoughts about it, have an idiosyncratic or individual character? Did his idea of a literary idea in some ways verge from the traditional one which he might have had from Dante or Geoffrey of Vinsauf? I say it did. And it differed in a way which scattered seed throughout the history of English letters. Ezra Pound said that 'no-one will ever gauge or measure English poetry until they know how much of it, how full a gamut of its qualities, is already *there on the page* of Chaucer'. I say that Chaucer's idea of an idea is what at base explains the important place he holds in English literary tradition.

And first: Chaucer seems to have introduced into the notion of rhetorical invention an element of chance. The best evidence of this comes about as a result of a mistranslation. Geoffrey of Vinsauf wrote that the poet is like a builder, that the 'measuring line of his mind first lays out the work'. Chaucer's text seems to have read (or he misread it as) *praemittitur* or *praemittetur* instead of *praemetitur*, for he translated it 'sends out':

> For everi wight that hath an hous to founde
> Ne renneth naught the werk for to bygynne
> With rakel hond, but he wol bide a stounde,
> And sende his hertes line out fro withinne,
> Aldirfirst his purpos for to wynne.[1]

And Chaucer embroidered on Geoffrey by adding 'Aldirfirst his purpos for to wynne'. It appears that Chaucer here makes a sort of philological Freudian slip: he begins with Geoffrey's metaphor (the standard medieval one) about planning and building a house, and without discarding the metaphor—for he returns to it later, in III.530, when he says of Pandarus's plan 'This tymbur is al redy up to frame'—he has him *send out* his heart's line to *win his purpose*. The builder's plumbline in his original becomes something much closer to a fisherman's line. The act of planning in his original becomes something much closer to a lucky accident, 'winning'—as we would say, 'getting' or 'catching'—something. And the thing

---

[1] *Troilus* I. 1065–1069. Quotations are from *The Works of Geoffrey Chaucer*, ed. F. N. Robinson (Cambridge, Mass., 1957).

caught is not the *archetypus* of his original but a 'purpose'—as we would say, an 'intention'.

This initial act of 'winning a purpose' seems to have troubled Chaucer enough at least that his anxiety about it found its way into some of his works. In his early poems, as critics have shown in detail,[1] he reveals himself casting about for material, hoping to find or 'win' something out of his dream life or reading or experience which he could use in his poems. In *The House of Fame*, when the Dantean eagle escorts him to the houses of Fame and Rumor, we find him in search of 'tidings': we learn that the mother of tidings is chance ('Aventure', 1982f.), and we hear the poet explain his presence in the House of Rumor to an unidentified questioner:

> . . . That wyl y tellen the,
> The cause why y stonde here:
> Somme newe tydynges for to lere,
> Somme newe thinges, y not what—
> Tydynges, other this or that,
> Of love, or suche thynges glade.
> For certeynly, he that me made
> To comen hyder seyde me
> Y shulde bothe here and se
> In this place wonder thynges.
> But these be no suche tydynges
> As I mene of.
>   (1884–1895)

These 'things' or 'tidings' he has been promised—tidings of love, it was suggested earlier (675ff.)— are going to fall into his hands by chance: there is nothing he can do to drum them up. The notion is borne out in all of Chaucer's major poems: he does represent the source of each poetic conception as something found or 'won'— in the dream-visions a dream inspired by a book or story, in the *Troilus* the 'old book' by Lollius, in *The Canterbury Tales* a gathering on a pilgrimage which simply 'befell' and a sequence of

---

[1] Notably, for example, J. A. W. Bennett, *Chaucer's* Book of Fame: *An Exposition of 'The House of Fame'* (Oxford, 1968).

tales which begins and seems to proceed 'by aventure or sort or cas'.

This lucky accident, this finding or catching a purpose, happens in an interior or 'mentalistic' realm which exists in time, in history. Poems and poets live and die in the House of Fame; but the raw material of their poems, 'tidings', comes from the House of Rumor. This seems to suggest that poems originate in what one hears but the real locus of a poem is not on pages or in books but in the actual realm in which poems survive, in tradition. The heart's line goes *out*, but with luck it draws something in. The purpose won is not the finished poem but its idea; it will be shaped by and will exist in a tradition. The conception is not the same as Northrop Frye's or Harold Bloom's notion that poems are made of other poems: Chaucer suggests that poems are made of a common basic stuff, 'tidings', and that poets survive or do not survive alongside other poets. A poetic tradition is at base only a grab-bag of verbal tidbits ('tidings'); whatever direction it has is owing to Fame—to prestige or reputation. As there is an element of chance in poetic invention, there is an element of chance in poetic tradition—in the survival and influence of a poem. Poems exist in Fame's house, a mental realm which is a castle in the sky built on ice, and the names of 'famous folks' engraved in the ice are melting on the sunny side. It is perhaps the most astonishing image in Chaucer—an allegory, as it actually is, of the world of consciousness seen diachronically, the intercommunion of mind as an historical entity, where tidings are not necessarily true and survival not necessarily just, where what does survive is to the north and in the shade, protected for a time from the mutability of the natural order.

While his predecessors likened the process of making a poem to that of building a house, Chaucer thus represented the realm of poetry as itself a house. And he imagined another kind of house from which we get poems, the House of Rumor, and likened it to 'the Domus Dedaly/That Laboryntus cleped ys' (1920f.). Daedalus, the mythical builder of the labyrinth, was the architect or builder *par excellence*. And the labyrinth he created, that mythic house, was in the Middle Ages itself a symbol of building. In churches and Gothic cathedrals especially in Italy and France we find a labyrinth or maze inlaid as a mosaic on a wall or pavement. In some cases the architect of a Gothic cathedral inscribed his name in the centre of the labyrinth which stood at the centre of the cathedral floor: the builder symbolized God the creator and the labyrinth symbolized creation. It is widely believed, but not proved, that the pavement labyrinths of Gothic cathedrals were used as substitute pilgrimages—the penitent crawled on his knees along the unicursal way from the entrance of the labyrinth to its centre, which was called *ciel* or *Jérusalem*; in France pavement labyrinths were called *Dédales* or *chemins de Jérusalem*.[1] So while the labyrinth symbolized the created universe, it also symbolized the pilgrimage of human life, the world. In appropriating the figure of the labyrinth to describe the House of Rumor, Chaucer seems to have suggested that the source of poems, this interior or mentalistic realm, is the world itself, whose end is to be subsumed in the timeless universe. A poetical idea ultimately comes out of a remembered or reported experience *of the world*; its meaning is complete only at the end of time, when the world is complete. Poems are by their very nature among the transitory things of this world.

This 'House of Rumor' which is like the labyrinth turns out to be a giant wicker cage whirling about, which both holds and filters tidings. The centrality of tidings in this conception of poetry explains why the House of Rumor has the final and climactic position. These tidings are passed about by word of mouth, they become bloated and distorted in the telling, and some escape through the doors or cracks of the House of Rumor. It might be said that they are to poems what phonemes are to words or morphemes to sentences. So if we want to know Chaucer's idea of a poetical idea we have to know what he meant by tidings. According to the OED a tiding is something that has happened, an event—and more often the announcement of such an event, in other words a piece of news. In Chaucer it seems to mean the announcement of such news by word of mouth or by letter.

[1] See W. H. Matthews, *Mazes and Labyrinths: Their History and Development* (rpt. Dover, 1970), esp. chap. 9.

Tidings don't bear a one-to-one relation to the events they report —you can have more than one tiding for one event, and you can have a tiding for a non-event: Chaucer twice (in *The House of Fame*, line 2098, and the Manciple's Tale, line 360) makes it indisputably clear that a tiding is a tiding whether it is true or false. Thus he finds in the House of Rumor the most notorious kinds of liars—'shipmen and pilgrimes/With scrippes bret-ful of lesinges,/ Entremedled with tydynges' (2123ff.), and he adds, 'many a thousand tymes twelve/Saugh I eke of these pardoners . . .' But a tiding can be true. Chaucer believed poems are made of tidings but you can't say he believed they are made of *lies*—they are made of reports whose objective truth is neither here nor there.

In this Chaucer was taking a radical position. Where medieval rhetoric held that poetry, or the idea of a poem, originates in the interior world of ideas, he held that poetry has its origin in rumour, in spoken language. In Chaucer's uses of the term a tiding can 'befall' or 'come' but otherwise it is something you 'say', 'tell', or (most often) 'hear'. Behind it is something that happened or is said to have happened. Tidings never come from reading: if you are a poet and you are looking for tidings, you put aside your book, as indeed Chaucer does in all his dream-visions. But from the book he goes direct to fantasy, not 'life'; the chitchat he hears can even come from talking birds. In pointing to the basic relation of poetry to the spoken language Chaucer seems to have had in mind not the stream of speech as it exists in objective reality but the stream of speech as it exists in our thoughts—what Vigotsky called 'inner speech'.[1]

The notion is important because in *The House of Fame* Chaucer introduces a theory of speech based on the physics of his day. The eagle who lectures the recalcitrant poet explains that speech is sound, that sound is broken air, and that air is the element which

[1] See 'Thought and Speech', in *Psycholinguistics*, ed. S. Saporta and J. R. Bastian (New York, 1961), pp. 509–35. On Chaucer's sense of this see my essay 'Experience, Language, and Consciousness: *Troilus and Criseyde*, II, 596–931', in *Medieval Literature and Folklore Studies: Essays in Honor of Francis Lee Utley*, ed. Jerome Mandel and Bruce A. Rosenberg (New Brunswick, N.J., 1970), pp. 173–92.

by 'kyndely enclynyng' goes up. The result is that if we are to inquire about tidings or fame we must examine the places in the sky where speech goes: we must observe speech in the abstract. The helter-skelter process we observe is presented in a retrospective structure—we observe Fame first; then the stuff of which Fame is made, Rumor; then the stuff of which Rumor is made, tidings. What we learn is that poems are made of tidings which are compounded of truth and falsehood (2108) and which are given names and durations by Fame (2110–2114). The reputations of poems and poets are made of tidings too. There is no reason or justice to the process by which fame is achieved or not achieved: the goddess Fame is as capricious as the goddess Fortune, who is, we learn, her sister (1547). The fame of former nations and heroes is held up by writers (1429–1519), but the fame of the writers themselves is in their names (for names are engraved on the very foundations of Fame's house) and in oral traditions (for minstrels and such are displayed on its outer walls). The writers in Fame's house are grouped by nation, whereas the purveyors of oral tradition were presented in a jumble (1184–1281). This wondrous world in the sky is really the poet's mind—memory is the preserving principle, and it is true we do remember writers one way and speakers or performers another, for writing preserves but petrifies while oral traditions change with the times.

Chaucer is very explicit in saying that the world he flies to is his mind. He says this in two key places, the proems to Books II and III. In the proem to Book II he figures thought as a writer and dreams as writings preserved in the treasury of his brain:

O Thought, that wrot al that I mette,
And in the tresorye hyt shette
Of my brayn, now shal men se
Yf any vertu in the be . . . (523–526)

In the proem to Book III he calls upon 'vertu'—'devyne vertu'—to 'shewe now/That in myn hed ymarked ys' (1101–1102) and says this means 'The Hous of Fame for to descryve' (1105). Even the House of Rumor turns about as 'swyft as thought' (1924). We are to find, 'ymarked' in his head, what Thought has written there, in this very dream which he has now written down: an account of 'art poetical', of its origin and duration in a mentalistic realm. When he says in this same passage 'Nat that I wilne for maistrye/Here art poetical be shewed' (1094–1095), the emphasis is on 'maistrye'. He means he *will* 'show art poetical', but not 'for maistrye'. He means he will show it for what he has to say about it, not to show off his own cleverness: he will 'do no diligence/To shewe craft, but o sentence' (1099–1100). Everything that follows in Book III is in the world of the mind: every speech that finds its way to this place retains the image of its speaker (1070–1083) the uttering mind is not separable from the utterance even if (presumably) that mind has only passed on a 'tiding', for tidings do change in passing from mouth to mouth.

This image of the poet's sense of tradition is a different view from the modern one which holds that the individual poet responds to the burden of the past and wrestles single-handed with the anxiety of influence, and to my mind it comes closer to the truth at least for medieval poets: the individual poet has his niche in a historical structure among other poets of his age and nation, and they will survive as part of the structuring together. Chaucer, living just at the dawn of the classical revival, expresses the idea by naming writers of the ancient cultures.

What this must mean is that poets rise or fall, live or die, on the sheer grounds of whether anyone is reading them and talking about them. The fate of a poem depends on its readers, and on different *kinds* of readers. Chaucer acknowledges this in *The Canterbury Tales* when he makes the famous reference to turning over the leaf and choosing another tale. If you don't like 'harlot-rie', you will find enough, he tells us, 'grete and smale', of 'storial thyng that toucheth gentillesse', and 'eek moralitee and hoolynesse'. This sounds like a list of genres—we are going to hear fabliaux, romances, and saints' legends or sermons—but the position implied about the nature of genres, a position which could deserve a modest renaissance in our own time, is that genres are not mere classifications imposed after the fact, nor Platonic ideas or universals, but *kinds* which grow out of a dynamic relationship between tellers and hearers—tales, or for that matter tidings, exist because they appeal to different kinds of readers or hearers, and those readers or hearers naturally fall into social groups. Each of the tales told on the Canterbury pilgrimage is from this point of view a tiding—a bit of *lore*—heard and reported by a pilgrim for those pilgrims who share common attitudes and values with him; and then all the tales are 'rehearsed' in sequences by the narrator for various readerships or for a readership with a taste for various kinds of tales.

Now it is just in these sequences of tidings, re-told by the narrator and re-heard by us, that we see embodied in *The Canterbury Tales* what was foreshadowed in *The House of Fame*. The objective truth of a tiding is of no consequence; when it is reified in a tale or a poem or a book it becomes a *thing*, or part of a thing —and 'thing' was a Middle English word for 'poem'—that exists in the world for a certain time. As part of such a thing, every tiding is true in one way or another. You have to *look* for the truth of a tiding, and not all tidings are true in the same way, but every tiding is authentic: either it has a real event behind it or else it 'wexeth lyk the same wight/Which that the word in erthe spak' (*HF*, 1076f.). It tells us something but the burden is on us to know what that something is. St Augustine said that if you have an image of a man in a mirror it cannot be a true image without being a false man. And he went on to ask, 'if the fact that they are false in one respect helps certain things to be true in another respect, why do we fear falseness so much and seek truth as such a great good? . . . Will we not admit that these things make up truth itself, that truth is so to speak put together from them?'[1]

In *The Canterbury Tales* Chaucer took this position about the relative truth of fictions. And he made his position clear by setting up the Parson as a foil. The Parson in his Prologue isn't smart enough to see what Chaucer saw. 'Thou getest fable noon ytoold for me,' he barks. He takes the position of naïve realism—he thinks all fables are lies and all lies are bad. He thinks you have to have 'whete' or otherwise you will have 'draf'. Chaucer's idea was the reverse. If you tell a tale, true or false, your choice of the tale

[1] *Soliloquia*, II.10 (*PL* 32:893), trans. mine.

and your motive and manner in telling it tells a truth about you. There is a truth somewhere, but it is relative, various—and partial. Chaucer never claims to possess the *whole* truth. The Parson doesn't either, to be sure, for he puts himself 'under correccioun'. But the Parson implies that with 'correccioun' one could at least in theory express the whole truth in a prose treatise. Chaucer makes the opposite implication. He quotes St Paul that all that is written is written for our doctrine and says 'that is my intent'. The question that remains is of course how we *get* the doctrine out of all that is written. And Chaucer's answer, very unlike the Parson's but not unlike St Paul's, is that it is up to us to find it in our own way. We use the foolish things of the world to confound the wise. Part of Chaucer's idea is simply that no literary idea can approach its full potential of 'poetic truth' unless it engages the reader's interest and enlists his participation. It demands of us an act of will, for the truth of a poem is in *our* idea of it.

Now it is undeniable that one way of gaining the truth from a poem was to read it allegorically. This was to an extent true of medieval notions about reading; it was much truer after Chaucer's time and well into the seventeenth century that poems, especially pagan poems, were understood to be 'mysteriously meant'. All of this has been documented by Don Cameron Allen.[1] But there was another notion about poetic truth, in some ways harder for us to grasp because it is more familiar to us—because it has never died and because we take it for granted. And this was Chaucer's idea. But it is not an idea in the usual sense—not something he thought consciously but something he *did*. It was what we would call a feeling: Chaucer seems to have had a feeling that at the heart of any literary work is something that has happened, or at least been told, a 'tiding'. True or false, some tidings catch our fancy and some do not—who knows why? Chaucer followed his instincts and acted on this feeling. We might compare the way most of us would describe our 'idea' of how to teach a class or write a paper: we do what works for us, and what works for us *is* our idea even

[1] *Mysteriously Meant: The Rediscovery of Pagan Symbolism and Allegorical Interpretation in the Renaissance* (Baltimore and London, 1970).

though often enough we cannot state that idea except by inventing examples or telling anecdotes. I am claiming then that at the heart of Chaucer's idea was a feeling of which he was not perhaps fully conscious but which *I* am able to articulate—a most outrageous claim, as it may seem, the very daughter of Fatuity and Delusion—but I am not alone in thinking it. On the contrary, I am indebted to that scholar who has dealt most penetratingly with Chaucer's use of medieval rhetoric, Robert Payne. As Payne has recently reminded us,[1] Chaucer knew that no artist can provide what he thinks are the necessary and adequate aims for poetry unless he thinks he knows what he is doing. But, Payne adds, Chaucer also knew 'that for even the best of men, what one thinks he is doing is never quite exactly what he is doing'.

Then if the heart of Chaucer's idea was in what he did more than in what he thought, what did he do? It used to be said that what he did was to break with convention and go direct to life; now, for a generation, scholars have been toiling to prove that he broke with life and went direct to convention. This counter-trend has produced a sort of universal rule of thumb that nothing in Chaucer is what it seems. The Pardoner is really Faux-Semblant, Chauntecleer is the friars, Pandarus is the devil, the Wife is La Vieille. If this had been so, how could we explain the enthusiasm of readers in the centuries after Chaucer's death for Chaucer's pilgrims and tales, much the same pilgrims and tales we feel enthusiasm for—the Pardoner, who attracted the anonymous author of the *Tale of Beryn*, or the Wife's tale, which attracted John Milton as a study of 'the discommodities of marriage', as he called it, or the Squire's tale, which attracted Spenser and Milton? Their enthusiasm argues powerfully in favour of Chaucer's idea, whose universal rule of thumb was that everything is *exactly and only what it seems*, that every utterance is *exactly and only what it says*. The Pardoner is only the Pardoner; Chauntecleer, Chauntecleer; Pandarus, Pandarus; the Wife, the Wife. We must practise a rule of abstinence, must do as the Nun's Priest counsels—keep our eyes open and our mouths shut. Chaucer seems to have believed that

---

[1] 'Chaucer and the Art of Rhetoric', in *Companion to Chaucer Studies*, ed. Beryl Rowland (Oxford Univ. Press, 1968), p. 53.

you can get tidings, can 'tell a tale after a man', can 'rehearse' it in such a way that people will react as Harry Bailly and the pilgrims react, by laughing, by being dumbfounded, by arguing, by calling a halt, by telling another tale. What causes this reaction is the uniqueness and delimitedness, the authenticity, of each personage and utterance. This authenticity is what *we* perceive as Chaucer's irony: Chaucer teases us—or we tease ourselves—into supposing that things are something bigger and the characters something more than what they seem, and the irony is that they are not. They are always and only themselves; it is for us to make of them what we will.

Among those unique and delimited personages the slipperiest of them is Chaucer himself, the gatherer of tidings who appears in his own works as observer, speaker, and writer. In the present century our attitude to him has been shaped by Kittredge's argument that 'a naif Collector of Customs would be a paradoxical monster'.[1] It was a very witty remark, and Kittredge went on to argue that 'naivete is incompatible with a sense of humor'. 'If I am artless,' Kittredge said, 'I may make you laugh; but the sense of humor, in that case, is yours, not mine.' In another mood, and another lecture, Kittredge seems to have acknowledged that Chaucer understood and capitalized on this circumstance.[2] And the most subtle treatments of the 'narrator' have acknowledged this: given all the formalistic distinctions we can make between the man and the artist, or among the man, the pilgrim, and the poet, we never know positively which we are hearing, and are not meant to know. We engage ourselves with a disembodied voice which is written down and which we must pretend to hear. Seen this way Chaucer *is* a 'naif' and therefore *is* a paradoxical monster —we may assume, a very smart and knowing one. There is nothing after all in this poetry except tidings. And Chaucer's irony is not only in the voice: it is the essential irony of all tidings, the irony we experience every time we pick up a newspaper, read the weather report, or the stock market quotations, the latest scandal or emergency or unsolved murder or incipient war: we

[1] *Chaucer and His Poetry* (Cambridge, Mass., 1915), p. 45 f.
[2] E.g., *ibid.*, pp. 75 f., 160 f., 183-5.

understand what the tidings are and say, but puzzle over what they mean, what outcome or import they may have. Tidings are news, and the news is by nature ironic: we never understand it until it becomes history, but then it is no longer news, and we have historiography to contend with—itself an ironic circumstance.

Seen from this point of view, the Wife is an ironic figure because she is *not* La Vieille or *die ewige Weibliche* or the 'old dance' or any such thing—she is always and only the Wife. We do not understand her. She does not understand herself. Chaucer does not understand her and does not claim to. When he says she had five husbands 'withouten oother compaignye in youthe', the irony is that he means exactly and only that: 'without other company in youth'. Things are after all not what they seem, but this is because the remark may *seem* to mean 'outside of other company in youth' yet it does not necessarily mean that. It can equally mean 'without having other company in youth'. The OED cites it as an obsolete sense 'intermediate between senses I and III', which I suppose does get at Chaucer's effect. It is a tiding; we may make of it what we can. And perhaps the best we can make of it is that our actual experience of the world is precisely of this kind. If you met the Wife, wouldn't you wonder what she'd been like before that first marriage? Isn't it just that fomenting time of her life which she would not tell you anything about—would probably not fully understand herself, or remember? And isn't one explanation of her complicated marital history the possibility that in her format-ive youth she *was* without company? What we don't know is what is interesting and important here. The phrase is pregnant with meaning but the only scholarly way to decide that meaning is to follow the OED and create an intermediate category—which is to call it ambiguous. We perceive such ambiguities as ironic, but the irony is *in us*—it is in our response to Chaucer's idea, which was to express accurately those tidings which experience and the world presented to him. If you call it deadpan or tongue-in-cheek or ironic you are only acknowledging, what is surely true, that Chaucer knew he could count on this 'ironic' response in us, or most of us. Irony is an acquired taste, and not everyone acquires it. So Chaucer's idea was risky and theatrical, 'distanced', and highly disciplined. It calls upon a frame of mind in us—anticipates that frame of mind and in part inculcates it. It is not a 'strategy', for strategy by definition manipulates. It is rather a stance which invites and permits.

It was this part of his idea, this stance, which Chaucer bequeathed to English literature. It has been the mainstay of English fiction, the essence of the drama and the novel as they were to develop. The artist effaces or disguises himself, throws attention on the 'realities' of his story, the 'true history' he purports to relate. But the authenticity he offers is not in realities or history or even in tidings. It is in appearances, in the way things *seem*. It is therefore a wholly mentalistic or psychological phenomenon: the tiding reported by the writer and acknowledged by the reader can be true or false. It has its authenticity in inner experience—in the mentalistic world of Rumor and Fame. Fiction in this tradition deflects our attention to *seeming*: to the author's or narrator's mind, or to one character's mind, and always in some measure to the reader's mind. Its verisimilitude resides not in details but in the aura of the unknown and unknowable that pervades details and is the essence of 'tidings'. Chaucer appears to have grasped this principle before anyone else; but others grasped it too and later English writers may have found it elsewhere. Pound stated a precise historical fact when he wrote that what was to characterize English poetry 'is already there on the page of Chaucer', for he did not imply *post hoc ergo propter hoc*; he meant that Chaucer found it first.

Such an estimate of Chaucer's place in English letters, like Dryden's or Arnold's, makes Chaucer stand at the head of modern (as opposed to medieval) literature, and I espouse this view. But there is another side to Chaucer's idea of an idea which makes his abstemious way of putting tidings on paper altogether compatible with medieval thought: he acknowledged that it was all *only an idea*. In the last analysis tidings are noise, and while we may grasp a truth from the total experience of hearing or reading them, from the experience of contemplating *seeming*, the better way is silence. For this reason Chaucer always rejects in the end the very thing he is in search of. The alternative to the jumble of tidings is Troilus's distant laughter, the poet's silent adoration of the Daisy; at the end of *The Canterbury Tales*, before the Parson's loquacious discourse, in the Manciple's Tale, the talking crow is deprived of his ability to 'countrefete the speche of every man . . . whan he sholde telle a tale' (134–135), Phebus the god of poetry destroys his harp, and the audience is bombarded with a collection of proverbs on the virtue of silence. Chaucer's idea of a literary idea included the recognition that a work of literature is only one of many things in this world, that it lives in an inner world of ideas and sententiae and memories which alone give duration and authenticity to tidings, and that this inner world too will vanish in the end.

IV

The English Romance in the Fifteenth Century

DEREK PEARSALL

COMPARATIVELY little has been written on the English romance in the fifteenth century, and the standard work on the English verse-romances, that of Dieter Mehl,[1] is specifically confined to the romances of the thirteenth and fourteenth centuries. There are good reasons for this concentration of emphasis, in that the majority of the verse-romances are thought to have been composed before about 1400. There are also less good reasons, amongst which one might mention an over-preoccupation, particularly in earlier writings on the romances, with the origins of stories and story-motifs, and also the assignation of a more than usually arbitrary significance to the date 1400. However, the more generous terms of chronological reference of the revision of Wells's *Manual*[2] offer encouragement for a study of the continuation and development of the traditions of romance-writing beyond 1400. It is a preliminary study of this kind that the present essay aims to provide, and one directed primarily to problems of authorship, audience and contemporary taste.[3]

Any study of 'romance' must offer some interim definition of the term, and the responsibility cannot be evaded here, even though the contents of the revised *Manual* are accepted as the *de*

[1] D. Mehl, *The Middle English Romances of the Thirteenth and Fourteenth Centuries* (London, 1968; first published as *Die mittelenglischen Romanzen des 13. und 14. Jahrhunderts*, Heidelberg, 1967).

[2] *A Manual of the Writings in Middle English 1050–1500*, ed. J. B. Severs, Fascicule 1: Romances (New Haven, 1967).Wells's original *Manual* went up only to 1400. Romances mentioned in the present essay without reference to a specific edition are cited from the latest authoritative edition listed in the Bibliography of the revised *Manual*, which is also the source for information on MSS.

[3] Romances from Scotland and the extreme north of England are not dealt with here, since they constitute to a large extent a separate study.

facto materials of the study. The paragraph of definition at the beginning of the *Manual* (p. 11) is too elaborate for comfort but it might be pared of its inessentials to produce a definition of romance as 'a narrative intended primarily for entertainment, in verse or prose, and presented in terms of chivalric life'. No part of this definition should be pressed too hard, but it is adequate to exclude, for instance, on good grounds, such a work as the verse-translation by Gilbert Banester (c. 1445) of the story of *Guiscardo and Ghismonda* from Boccaccio's *Decameron* (ed. EETS 205). Nevertheless, there are some inconsistencies, given this definition, in the selection of the 115 romances enumerated in the *Manual*. Some translations by Caxton which are romances by the strictest definition are excluded because of prior affiliations in the structure of the *Manual* as a whole. Likewise, some works are drawn into the enumeration solely because they are associated with one of the traditional 'matters'; such are the short prose and verse lives of *Joseph of Arimathia* printed in the early sixteenth century (no. 42), which are simple hagiography, and the so-called *Dublin Alexander Epitome* (no. 70), which is a mere string of anecdotes of the *Dicts and Sayings* kind. All these are in prose. A harder test of definition is provided by the ballads, six of which are included in the enumeration because of their association with genuine romances.[1] The dividing line between romance and ballad is blurred, as will appear from some of the romances we are to deal with here, but it is real enough, and in the last analysis a ballad is formally identifiable through its brevity and verse-form and through certain patterns of repetitive phrasing. With these inconsistencies removed, which mostly concern the rather loose selection of 17 prose romances included in the *Manual*, one would be left with a total of 92 verse-romances in Middle English.

Yet even here there is still inconsistency, for the enumeration conceals some contradictory decisions on the part of the different contributors to the *Manual* as to what constitutes a numerable unit. For instance, the two poems on *The Carl of Carlile* (nos.

---

[1] Viz. *Hind Horn* (no. 3), *Guy and Colbrond* (8), *The Legend of King Arthur* (17), *Lancelot du Lake* (22), *King Arthur's Death* (24), *King Arthur and King Cornwall* (37).

28–9), which are related, and the three versions of *Landeval* (nos. 89–91), which are comparatively closely related, are enumerated separately, while genuinely independent versions of *Octavian, Alexander, Guy of Warwick, Generydes* and *The Siege of Jerusalem* are numbered as one romance. Further inconsistencies could be mentioned, but briefly, if one applies a single criterion of what constitutes an independent romance, the number of verse-romances in Middle English is 95. Of these 95, only 30 occur in copies that pre-date the Thornton manuscripts (c. 1440), even though 61 at least would be regarded as of fourteenth-century provenance.[1] In broad terms, if it were not for copies made well after the turn of the century, half the fourteenth-century romances would be unknown.

I

This is the first point to stress about the fifteenth century, that it is the great age of fourteenth-century romance, not because it instils in us a proper gratitude to fifteenth-century scribes, but because the way a work is read and used contributes significantly to its place in literary history, and because the work of copying is, with these poems, often a work of re-composition. The surviving manuscripts of individual poems, particularly of the most popular romances,[2] show a wide range of textual variation, far wider than can be explained by the processes of scribal transmission, and it is clear that many of the texts we have are in part the product of oral transmission. Whoever composed these poems, whether bookshop

[1] H. S. Bennett, in his essay on 'The Production and Dissemination of Vernacular Manuscripts in the Fifteenth Century', *The Library*, 5th Series, 1 (1946–7), 167–78, says that 65 (out of 84) romances appear only in 15th century copies. The agreement of his 65 with mine is only apparent, since I count a larger total and allow a larger penumbra of palaeographical doubt in the early 15th century.

[2] Viz. *Bevis of Hamton, Guy of Warwick, Arthour and Merlin, Libeaus Desconus, Isumbras, Eglamour, Degare* and *Richard Coer de Lyon*. These are assumed to be the most popular because they exist in the largest number of MS copies (5 or more each). *Titus and Vespasian* (13 MSS) and *Roberd of Cisyle* (10 MSS) are even more popular on this reckoning, but they are to a large extent regarded as religious works, and are copied in a different kind of MS. *Gamelyn*, which appears in 26 MSS of the *Canterbury Tales*, is another exceptional case.

hacks, *disours* or clerics, they were evidently written for performance, and became to that extent the property of the *disours*. It is
their memories of a written text, modified in performance, that
provide, directly or indirectly, many of the extant copies.[1] A
lucid demonstration of this process of re-composition has been
made by Mills in his work on Thomas Chestre, especially his work
on the source-text of MSS A, N and P of *Libeaus Desconus*.[2] He
has shown that re-composition does not necessarily produce a
garbled text, that it may indeed merely reproduce the processes of
original composition, so that 'errors' may be survivals of a careless
original, while 'authentic variants' may be merely moderately
intelligent acts of rewriting by scribes who had the same equip-
ment and the same goals as the original composer.[3] The existence
of such texts demands from us a special kind of understanding, one
which recognizes a fluidity in the nature of a popular romance
analogous to that of a piece of medieval music. After the writing
down of the original poem, individual texts crystallize moments in
the poem's existence, in a process of change. The impulse to write
down a copy of a romance is nothing to do with an intention of
recording its perfected form—there is no sense that this is 'the
text' of the poem—and the process of change continues after the
poem is written down. Even the idea of a single text evolving is an
over-simplification, since each romance lies in a network of
intersecting developments, a phrase or motif being borrowed and
introduced here and there, as for instance MS Ashmole 61 of *Sir
Orfeo* introduces at the beginning six lines of spring-description
from *Arthour and Merlin*, or the source-text of MSS C and F of *Sir
Eglamour* introduces variations based on *Emare*. The lines describ-
ing the dragon (781–98) in the same CF source-text (which is

---

[1] On these and related matters, see A. C. Baugh, 'The Middle English
Romance: Some Questions of Creation, Presentation and Preservation',
Speculum 42 (1967), 1–31; 'Improvisation in the Middle English Romance',
Proceedings of the American Philosophical Society 103 (1959), 418–54.

[2] M. Mills, 'The Composition and Style of the "Southern" *Octavian, Sir
Launfal* and *Libeaus Desconus*,' *Medium Aevum* 31 (1962), 88–109; 'A Mediaeval
Reviser at Work', *ibid.* 32 (1963), 11–23; (ed.) *Libeaus Desconus*, EETS 261
(1969), Introduction.

[3] *Libeaus Desconus*, ed. Mills, Intro., pp. 15–16.

dependent on oral transmission) are some of the liveliest in the poem, and demonstrate clearly that re-composition does not always of itself involve deterioration, though of course the further processes of scribal transmission will produce a garbled effect in the extant copy, as in the Lincoln's Inn MS 150 of *Kyng Alisaunder*.[1]

To this extent one could claim for the fifteenth century a continued role in the production of popular romances: a fifteenth-century text of a fourteenth-century poem may be in part a fifteenth-century poem. Widespread copying of the old romances combined with paucity of new composition suggest that the demand for popular romance was still strong but was mostly satisfied by variations on a few favourite models.[2] At this point one might begin to look for developments, in this process of re-composition, particularly characteristic of fifteenth-century taste. It is at first difficult to find them. One might conjecture, for instance, that some later texts of *Bevis of Hamton*, in so far as one can disentangle their readings from Kölbing's footnotes, show an increased fondness for violent and gruesome detail, as of guts trailing about the feet or bodies dismembered,[3] but it is hard to make generalizations about taste on the basis of differences which may be chance survivals of random variations. One point, perhaps, that could be made about *Bevis*, the textual history of which is more complex than that of any other Middle English romance, is that the range of textual variation is greatest in the most exciting scenes, such as Bevis's escape from prison (1655–1720) or the fight in London's streets (4313–4582). It may be that it was in these passages that the *disour* felt he could improvise most effectively— in other words, improvisation was not always a matter of mere

[1] For the examples cited here, see *Sir Orfeo*, ed. A. J. Bliss (Oxford, 1954), p. 46; *Sir Eglamour of Artois*, ed. Frances E. Richardson (EETS 256, 1965), pp. 116, 140; *Kyng Alisaunder*, ed. G. V. Smithers, vol. 2 (EETS 237, 1957), pp. 11–12.

[2] Of the 199 MS copies (including fragments) of the 90 relevant verse-romances (i.e. excluding four that appear only in prints, and *Gamelyn*), 67 are of 12 romances, and 52 are of the 8 mentioned above (note 2, p. 58); these 8 also account for half the 50 or so early prints.

[3] E.g. 517–18, 802, 1251–1310, 1315–30, 4233–40, in the late grouping formed by MS Chetham 8009 (c. 1450) and the Pynson print (c. 1503), Kölbing's M. and O.

necessity—and one might speculate too that certain episodes in a well-known romance acquired a degree of notoriety and the *disour* was expected to grace them with touches of his own.

In the main, the processes of re-composition argue for a continuity of taste, in which few specific directions can be isolated. The identification of 'Traciens' with Winchester is found only in the Auchinleck text of *Sir Orfeo* (line 25), and looks to us like a naïve 'popular' addition; but the omission of the detail in the two fifteenth-century manuscripts of the poem may be as much because a later *disour* found it over-learned as because he found it naïve. However, certain trends can be tentatively recognized. One is the adaptation of romances for a reading public. John Thornton, for instance, in his text of *Sir Eglamour* in Lincoln Cathedral Library MS 91, makes many arbitrary divisions in the poem, anticipating the practice in prose romance and suggesting an appeal to the eye rather than to the ear; he also rationalizes the syntax and dilutes the sense by the addition of more complicated conjunctions, and adds many extra-metrical *dixit*'s such as are superfluous for the audience of a practised *disour* but welcome to the reader.[1] Both in *Eglamour* and *Sir Degrevant*, which he copies in the same manuscript, he omits (or does not add) the characteristic fitt-ending, 'Make we mery, so haue we blysse!/For þys ys þe fyrst fytte, iwys . . .' (*Eglamour*, 343–4). These fitt-endings, however, are usually extra-metrical or detachable, and their presence or absence is no proof of the destination of a text. On the whole it can be taken as a general rule that references within a romance to a listening audience do not provide a certain indication of the actual mode of delivery, since some dramatization of the author-audience relationship is characteristic of nearly all literature. On the other hand, references to the written text and the private reader are not likely in a romance designed for performance, since they are not appropriate to the dominant relationship.

A second trend that can be identified is towards a greater degree of sophistication, though the movement is very relative. The scribe of MS Harley 525 of *The Seege of Troye*, for instance, seems

[1] *Sir Eglamour*, ed. cit., p. xvi.

concerned not only to remove from the text all references to a listening audience and all the characteristic *chevilles* of the popular entertainer, but also to correct and improve its content[1]. So, in the description of the Judgment of Paris, he replaces the 'four ladies of Elfen land' (508), who appear in the other manuscripts as Saturn, Jupiter, Mercury and Venus, with the correct three, Juno, Pallas and Venus. Again, the text of *Guy of Warwick* in Cambridge University Library MS Ff. ii. 38, which is usually accepted to be an independent fifteenth-century version,[2] 'improves' on earlier versions (and on the Anglo-Norman original) by adding an account of the dubbing of Guy and his friends (387–422), touched with picturesque detail and chivalric high-mindedness. One's sense that this is a significant innovation is reinforced in a later episode where Guy wages his glove before duke Otho in fashionable challenge (2659) instead of hitting him in the teeth, as in the original and in all earlier versions (e.g. Auchinleck, 2745), even though the subsequent passage is preserved where Guy and Otho have to be separated by the onlookers, which is irrelevant in the new non-violent context. Detail of this kind, with its emphasis on the external forms of chivalry, 'tended to proliferate as the practical function of knighthood disappeared',[3] and the changes in *Guy* may be a straw in the fifteenth-century wind. However, the evidence of the text as a whole is too ambiguous to admit of any general conclusion about a more sophisticated level of address or a more sophisticated audience. Some of the coarseness and violence of the earlier versions is toned down,[4] but there is no radical change in atmosphere and the mode of address is still that of the

---

[1] *The Seege or Batayle of Troye*, ed. M. E. Barnicle (EETS 172, 1926), p. xxxvii; G. Hofstrand, *The Seege of Troye: A Study in the Intertextual Relations of the Middle English Romance 'The Seege or Batayle of Troye'*, Lund Studies in English, IV (1936; repr. 1967), pp. 121–40.

[2] The dating is primarily on the evidence of the date of the MS. The version is not completely independent, since two long passages (7261–8024, 8541–9874) correspond in detail to the 14th century MS Caius 107 (7445–8218, 8802–10231).

[3] A. B. Ferguson, *The Indian Summer of English Chivalry* (Durham, N.Ca., 1960), p. 17.

[4] E.g. 1029 (cf. Auchinleck, 1394), 3404 (Auch. 3651), 3656 (Auch. 3901). The corresponding passages in *Gui de Warewic* (ed. A. Ewert, 2 vols., Paris, 1932–3) are at lines 1289, 3629, 3903.

disour. It might be concluded that the fifteenth-century version is not really catering for an audience of greater sophistication but for one that likes to be thought so—the same audience, with a veneer of more 'informed' fashionable taste.

A similar point may be made about the early fifteenth-century *The Sowdone of Babylone*, the first romance that shows a knowledge of Chaucer. The echoes, which are quite specific, are concentrated in two passages: an introductory spring-description (41–6) which echoes the *General Prologue* ('Whan lovers slepen with opyn yze', 45), and an invocation to Mars (939–62), echoing the *Knight's Tale* and *Anelida and Arcite*, followed by a further spring-description (963–78) which owes something to *Piers Plowman*, perhaps, as well as Chaucer. The second spring-description is associated with a recommendation of spring as the time of love, and of love to all noble warriors, which is quite at odds with the gory battle-description that follows. Indeed, the borrowed materials are in general quite inappropriate to the raucous and popular tone of the romance as a whole. Given the fact that both passages are detachable from their context, that the second is a patch at the junction of two source-texts (the *Destruction de Rome* and *Fierabras*) and is in a syntactically disjointed 8-line stanza instead of the 4-line stanza of the rest of the poem, it seems clear that the poet or a reviser is giving his work a fashionable but clumsy face-lift. The effort to stir attention at a key transition in the narrative by an infusion from fashionable 'literary' models is paralleled in the Laud *Troy-Book* (3243–56), where alliterative verse is used in a similar way.

II

The development in fifteenth-century verse-romances of these trends towards a greater sophistication, stimulated by the influence of Chaucer and by the need to cater for the tastes of a growing reading public, will be traced in a moment, but first a word more needs to be said about the continuity of the more popular tradition. The evidence, as I have said, is in continued copying and re-composition, rather than new composition. The abridgement of *Ipomydon*, which restores the long and sophisticated tail-rhyme

version to the anonymity of popular form, may be cited as a
further example. But continuity is not possible without change,
and the change that takes place is a result of the growth of the
reading public. The traditional popular romances catered for a
general audience, not an exclusively 'popular' one; they provided
entertainment for the households of all but the aristocratic élite;
Chaucer knew them well. The gradual creaming-off of this
audience by the new Chaucerian poetry and by the new prose
romance, and the growth of private reading, leave the traditional
romance and the *disour* poised for a descent into the world of
more exclusively 'popular' entertainment. We should not
normally be privileged to witness the results of this descent, in
which written texts would be largely irrelevant, but the accidental
survival of the Percy folio (c. 1650), itself an accident of nature,
gives a unique opportunity to study late forms of genuinely
'popular' romance. The provenance of the romances in the
Percy folio is very varied,[1] and not all of them are based on bad
texts, but most betray the signs of their passage through the world
of low entertainment. *Lambewell*, for instance, is recognizably a
version of *Landeval*, but a farewell scene has been added so that the
hero can say goodbye to a predictable list of favourite Arthurian
worthies, including 'Sir Kay, that crabbed Knight' (37), and there
are later episodes where Lambewell betrays a true plebeian hesi-
tation before entering the bed of his faery mistress (173–9) and
where the two of them say goodbye in the hearty tones of some
latter-day Pyramus and Thisbe:

'Farewell, my hony, farwell my sweete!'
'Farewell, Sir Lambwell, till oft we meete!'   (203–4)

But the most interesting poems for the present purpose are the
group of Gawain-romances, presumed to be of fifteenth-century
provenance. Here we see romance in its last stages of development

---

[1] Some may be based on printed texts, as is the ballad of *King Arthur's Death*:
see C. B. Millican, 'The Original of the ballad "Kynge: Arthurs Death" in the
Percy Folio MS.', *PMLA* 46 (1931) 1020–24. Another MS, Douce 261 (dated
1564), contains fragmentary copies of four romances based on early printed
texts.

before ballad, and can often, furthermore, make comparisons with analogues of higher literary status. The Percy *Carle off Carlile*, for instance, is based on the original of the tail-rhyme *Syre Gawene and the Carle of Carelyle* in MS Porkington 10 of the National Library of Wales. It is more frank in its presentation of the tale's brutalities, it is reduced in scale, often by the expedient of omitting the tail-lines of the original, and it lacks the quasi-courtly expansions of the Porkington text, such as the account of the evening's entertainment at the Carl's castle (403–53). Superficially, it might seem to represent the form in decay. But despite its occasional fatuousness, the Percy text is an astute professional retelling of the story, which pays attention to motivation where necessary and stresses Gawain's courtesy, the point of the story, where appropriate. At the cost of seeming perverse, one might make the same point about *The Grene Knight* in the Percy folio, an abridgement of *Sir Gawain and the Green Knight*. The absurdity of the enterprise and the ludicrousness of the result are obvious, if what we are interested in is literary sophistication and the complex mapping of moral and social dilemma. But given the need to reduce the poem to a fifth of its original length, to make a half-hour recital, the job could have been worse done.

The third pair of poems, *The Marriage of Sir Gawaine* in the Percy folio, and *The Weddynge of Sir Gawen and Dame Ragnell* in MS Rawlinson C.86, offers more resistance to generalization. *The Marriage* bears no verbal relation to *The Weddynge* and the many lacunae in the text make it difficult to tell whether the story is told effectively. It is in ballad-metre, has much of the characteristic repetitive phrasing of ballad, and may be said to have passed over into the other life. *The Weddynge* is a peculiar poem, not an entertainer's poem at all. It is a careful and complete version of the story, quite full (855 lines), with continuous and consistent attention to the problem of behaviour it presents and to the reactions of the participants. There are none of the abrupt transitions and arbitrary juxtapositions so characteristic of romance in its reduced form. On the other hand, the writer seems to have little skill or experience in versifying and, though he aims at a six-line tail-rhyme stanza, the stanza-pattern often breaks down completely into a mixture of couplets and odd lines, and the desperate shifts to which he resorts to secure rhyme are readily apparent (e.g. 90–91, 94–5). He shows little familiarity with the tags and clichés of expression that made the handling of the stanza easy for the *disour*, and little understanding of the stress-patterning of the verse-line. The prayer for release from prison at the end of the poem (842–52) severs it altogether from the world of entertainment, and confirms that we are dealing with the work of an amateur.

A last and most interesting insight into the development of popular taste in romance is given by the two poems of *The Squyr of Lowe Degre*. The longer version appears only in sixteenth-century prints and should be dated not much earlier than the earliest (c. 1520). It is quite skilful in detail, bears no mark of oral address despite the popular nature of its materials, and is surely a late pastiche of the form, analogous to the Chaucerian *Court of Love* of about the same date – not a burlesque,[1] but a loving re-creation of the form with all its charm and absurdities. The lady's instructions to the Squire concerning his seven years' service (171–268) and the proper behaviour of a chivalrous knight ('And in your armure must ye lye', 183) and the king's promise to his grieving daughter of the elegant courtly existence that will be hers if she forgets her dead lover (739–52) are deliberate and nostalgic evocations of the world of romance. The poem is full of romantic furniture, and particularly of catalogues of the appurtenances of courtly life—trees and birds in the garden, foods, wines and musical instruments. We are closer to Sir Walter Scott than seems possible, but nostalgia for the world of romantic chivalry is not necessarily a late phenomenon: it is the twin of romantic chivalry itself.

The plot of the poem, by contrast, has some peculiar gaps in its motivation, nowhere more marked than in the climactic episode, where the Squire's urgent plea for admittance at the lady's bed-chamber door, where he is about to be ambushed by the wicked

---

[1] The view of K. S. Kiernan ('*Undo Your Door* and the Order of Chivalry', *Stud. in Philology* 70, 1973, 345–66), that the whole romance is a burlesque, is based on an insensitive modern reading of the poem.

steward's men (though he does not know this yet), is answered by the lady with a long unrelated speech which includes a summary of part of the plot of *Libeaus Desconus*. The repetition by the Squire of the command 'Undo youre dore', and the fact that Wynkyn de Worde's title for the poem in the early print is *Undo Youre Dore*, suggest that what we have here is a famous phrase from a famous story that has been inadequately integrated into a full romance-plot, which in turn is partly confused because the poet has attempted too rich a mix of story-motifs.[1] The Percy version is much shorter, about a sixth of the length of the print, and the motivation appears better, though the poem is so drastically abbreviated that questions of motivation do not get much chance to arise. Verbal parallels suggest that it is a shortened version of a common original,[2] adapted ruthlessly for ten-minute recital, with much movement in the direction of ballad, particularly in the repetitive phrasing of the exchange between the lady and her father (113–52).

III

In contrast to the developments which have just been described there is a movement in fifteenth-century verse-romance towards a greater sophistication and a more self-consciously 'literary' mode of treatment and address. Some hints of this movement can be found in a late fourteenth-century romance like the tail-rhyme *Ipomadoun*,[3] and others have already been picked up from fifteenth-century versions of earlier romances, but it is more decisively present, of course, in the new romances. *Partonope of Blois*, a lengthy and highly literate version of the twelfth-century French romance, is perhaps the best example. The subtleties of sentiment are very fairly preserved from the original, with some added emphasis on propriety and 'womanhede' in the heroine's role which may reflect the more rigid ethics of love of fifteenth-century

[1] Margaret Schlauch ('English Short Fiction in the 15th and 16th Centuries', *Stud. in Short Fiction* 3, 1965–6, 393–434), puts it more bluntly, suggesting that 'the poet has confused two stereotyped characters' (p. 397).

[2] *The Squyr of Lowe Degre*, ed. W. E. Mead (Boston, 1904), p. xxii.

[3] The alliterative romances are here excluded from consideration, since they seem to relate to a specific regional audience.

England,[1] but what distinguishes the English poem is the quality of its literary self-consciousness. There is extensive reminiscence of Chaucer, and a passage in the account of the tournament (11128–45) is close enough to the *Knight's Tale* to argue for immediate borrowing from a written copy.[2] The frequent passages of personal interpolation in the French original, in which the narrator makes a habit of relating the varied success in love of his characters to his own misfortunes with a disdainful mistress and his own timidity in love, are seized on with enthusiasm by the English redactor, who develops the role of the narrator with some wit.[3] The whimsical, petulant and timorous character he portrays is partly derived from Chaucer (he fears 'to hoppe so ferre ynne loue-ys dawnce', 2334) but is even more influenced by Gower's Amans. Elsewhere, particularly in the expanded version of the text represented in British Library MS Add. 35288, there are touches of visual realism (e.g. 2224, 3534) not in the original which suggest a lively imagination only partly absorbed in its work, and a strangely interpolated fabliau-type exemplum on jealousy (1761–83) in which the predominantly four-stress couplet of the poem gives way to a regular pentameter. The distance travelled from popular romance in this quasi-courtly poem, which may be dated to the second quarter of the fifteenth century, can be measured by comparing it with the fragmentary copy of an independent abridged popular version in the Vale Royal MS, which is an anthology of clichés from popular romance and lyric.

Partonope is quite uninfluenced by Lydgate, who should be

[1] See R. M. Spensley, 'The Courtly Lady in *Partonope of Blois*', *Neuphilologische Mitteilungen* 74 (1973), 288–91.

[2] See B. J. Whiting, 'A Fifteenth-Century English Chaucerian: The Translator of *Partonope of Blois*', *Mediaeval Studies* 7 (1945), 40–54. There are briefer notes by R. M. Smith in *Modern Language Notes* 51 (1936), 314 and by J. Parr, *ibid.* 60 (1945), 486–7.

[3] E.g. 2310 (Cf. French, 1871), 4453 (cf. 3423), 5269 (cf. 4048), 6759 (cf. 5503), 7635 (cf. 6261), 8669 (cf. 7119), 9664 (cf. 8057), 10121 (cf. 8397), 10883 (cf. 9201). The passage of a similar kind at 1209–52 seems to be an innovation (cf. French, 1131). An amusing *occupatio* at 6169–87 should be compared with the elaborate description in the French (4879–4922). The French *Partonopeu de Blois* is edited by J. Gildea, O.S.A., 2 vols., Villanova, Pa., 1967–8.

mentioned here as the poet who absorbed many of the traditions of historical romance into his own elaborately rhetoricated treatments of the stories of Troy and Thebes, and also as the poet whose influence is strongest in three other 'literary' romances of the fifteenth century. The ambitions of these romances, marked by their employment of the rhyme royal stanza and by their imitation of Lydgate's inflated style, are largely unrealized, and two at least of the poems are mere curiosities. John Metham's *Amorus and Cleopes* is a version of the Pyramus and Thisbe story equipped with borrowings from the Alexander-legend and Lydgate's *Troy-Book* and with a Christian ending in which the lovers are resurrected. Its technical and metrical incompetence make it almost unreadable, but Metham is interesting because he indicates clearly a new role for verse-romance: he writes, he says,

> To comfforte them that schuld falle in heuynes.
> For tyme on-ocupyid, qwan folk haue lytyl to do,
> On haly-dayis to rede, me thynk yt best so.   (2209–11)

Another comment that may be of interest, coming from one who seems to know the romances of chivalry so well, concerns the falling-off in the composition of new romances:

> Meruelyng gretly that noght nowe, as in eld tyme,
> Men do noght wryte knyghtys dedys; nowdyr in prose ner
>   ryme.   (2105–6)

However, not too much should be made of this as a comment on the contemporary literary situation, since Metham is referring to the celebration of the deeds of contemporary heroes and preparing the way for a tribute to his patron, Sir Miles Stapleton.

The other curiosity is *The Romans of Partenay*, a version of the early fifteenth-century French ancestral romance of the family of Partenay (or Lusignan), a composite of stock adventures woven round the central story of the serpent-maiden Melusine. Skeat suggests that the English author was a Poitevin with an English mother,[1] and some hypothesis of the kind may seem to be needed

[1] *The Romans of Partenay*, ed. W. W. Skeat (EETS 22, 1866; rev. 1899), p. xx.

to explain the extraordinary linguistic usage of the poem, in which un-English constructions abound (e.g. 'ryght ful preysingly', Prol. 96; 'doth treteth', 5718) and in which the syntax often collapses completely, as in a comment on John of Partenay, 'Off whom spokyng haue here in langage our' (6234). But the independent parts of the Prologue and Epilogue are much more clearly written and it may be that the poet was overcome by the problems of translation. The influence of Lydgate, too, is strong in the poem and the imitation of his tortured syntax and colourless polysyllabism is a further potent source of embarrassment for the poet.

Generydes, by contrast, is an accomplished professional performance. Its treatment of its French original (not now extant) shows a knowledge of Chaucerian literature and a concern for the etiquette of what is conceived of as courtly behaviour which argue again for a comparatively sophisticated audience. There is much attention to ceremonies of meeting and leave-taking, and occasionally an emphasis on ladylike notions of propriety reminiscent of *Partonope*, as for instance in the episode where the heroine Clarionas welcomes the decision of the laundress to escape with her, not because she will otherwise be betrayed, which is the point of story, but because

> ... ellys she had gon all womanles,
> Whiche had not ben hir honour in certayn. (4510–11)

These and other features, including extensive verbal parallelism, have led me to argue elsewhere that the poem is by the same author as *The Assembly of Ladies*,[1] and directed to the same kind of aspirant quasi-courtly audience. There is no trace of oral address in the poem, and features such as the invitation to look back through the text to check on a point of family relationship ('As here before in writeng may ye fynde', 4867) argue conclusively for a reading audience. On the other hand, though a reading audience can be presumed to be a fairly sophisticated one, one should

[1] 'The Assembly of Ladies and Generydes', Review of English Studies, n.s. 12 (1961), 229–37.

not be premature in assuming that a listening audience has to be an unsophisticated one, certainly not in the first half of the century. There is another independent version of *Generides*, in couplet form, which has every characteristic mark of oral address (e.g. 3769) and many reminiscences of popular romance but which is yet not radically less sophisticated or knowledgeable in its treatment of sentiment and manners. The fact that the battle-scenes are much more prolonged does not preclude a gentle audience. One might from this be in a position to argue that the same story could be presented in different ways not for different audiences but for the same audience in different circumstances.

Consideration of social and literary realities of this kind seems irrelevant to a discussion of the last of these fifteenth-century poems,[1] the couplet versions of the French prose *Merlin* and *Estoire del Saint Graal* made about 1425 by Henry Lovelich, the London Skinner, for his fellow-gildsman Henry Barton.[2] Lovelich's relationship with Barton is that of friend to friend, not poet to patron, and there is little likelihood that these two vast poems had any 'existence' beyond the act of friendship and compliment. There is a good deal of oral address, of no significance, and an odd interpolation in the *Merlin* (21581–96) includes some jocular by-play about the poet's need for a drink at this 'dry feast', but the joke is not very clear and is evidently a private one, not a reference to an actual performance.

IV

These verse-romances, even the best of them, have about them an air of obsolescence, not surprisingly, since their function is about to be taken over, and their audience annexed, by prose. The inevitability of this development, given the influence of continental models and the demands of an increasing reading public, is clear. One might conjecture that it was delayed for as long as it was only

---

[1] I have not mentioned the *Alexander-Cassamus* fragment in the semi-courtly Cambridge Univ. Lib. MS Ff.i.6. Though extracted from the Alexander-romance, *Les Voeux du Paon*, the episode is evidently chosen as an exercise in courtly debate not as a romance. The poem is written in the courtly ballade-stanza.

[2] See R. W. Ackerman, 'Herry Lovelich's *Merlin*', PMLA 67 (1952), 473–84.

because of a temporary respite granted to verse-romance by the prestige of Chaucer and Lydgate. The advantage of prose to a reading public as opposed to a listening audience was obvious,[1] and had long been recognized by French writers. The author of a thirteenth-century *dérimage*, that of the *Chevalier au Cygne*, explains his reasons thus:

> Et l'ai commenchié sans rime pour l'estore avoir plus abregier. Et si me sanle que la rime est moult plaisans et moult bele; mais moult est longue.[2]

He is of course referring to the longueurs of style and rhetorical amplification characteristic of verse-romance, not to the total length of the work, since prose romance, though comparatively abridged in treatment, can afford to be comprehensive in scope, because of the unlimited time available to the reader. It can, in a word, be 'compendious'. As a later French writer puts it, he has translated the old poems and 'reduitte en ceste prose' because princes and noblemen nowadays prefer prose to rhyme, 'pour le langaige quy est plus entier et n'est mie tant constraint'.[3]

The story of prose romance in fifteenth-century England is of a first few tentative steps followed by a torrent of Burgundian-style chivalric prose romances poured from Caxton's pen and press in the last quarter of the century. The first steps are worth retracing.

[1] For the association of prose with a reading public, and therefore with expanding literacy, see H. J. Chaytor, *From Script to Print* (Cambridge, 1945), p. 83; also R. Hirsch, *Printing, Selling and Reading 1450–1550* (Wiesbaden, 1967), p. 9. Of course the private reader is not the exclusive audience of prose romance, since a written text can always be read aloud. Sometimes this possibility is specifically mentioned, as in the preface to the prose *Guillaume d'Orange*: 'Qui d'armes, d'amours, de noblesse et de chevalerie, vouldra ouir beaux mos et plaisans racompter, mecte painne et face silence ou lise, qui lire vouldra . . .' (quoted in G. Doutrepont, *Les Mises en Prose des Épopées et des Romans Chevaleresques du XIVe au XVIe siècle*, Brussels, 1939, p. 381). Caxton, in his preface to *Godefroy of Boloyne*, exhorts 'alle noble men of hye courage to see this booke and heere it redde' (quoted in N. F. Blake, *Caxton's Own Prose*, London, 1973, p. 141). But reading aloud, which anyone can do at any time, is not the same as professional performance, which is a learnt art based on traditional forms.

[2] Quoted in Doutrepont, op. cit., p. 354.

[3] Preface to *L'Histoire de Charles Martel*, quoted in Doutrepont, op. cit., p. 45.

They begin with some straightforward redactions of the 'matter of antiquity', attempts to provide 'compendious' summaries of story-materials that were often becoming unmanageable in the bulky poetic versions. The impulse to composition is historical and factual rather than literary, and the works are 'romances' chiefly by association of content, but the functional efficiency of the new medium – new at least in this context—is already obvious. The prose *Life of Alexander* (c. 1430) in Thornton's Lincoln MS, based, like the alliterative *Alexander* poems, on a version of the *Historia de Preliis*, is a model of straightforward translation, unencumbered by ornament, amplification or authorial intervention. The prose versions of *The Siege of Thebes* and *The Siege of Troy* in MS Rawlinson D.82 (c. 1450) are equally well-written, in a rather more expansive style, one in fact that is sometimes reminiscent of Caxton's developed style in his later translations. The literary connections of the two translations are suggested by the presence in the same manuscript of an extract from Gower's *Confessio Amantis*, and proved in the case of the *Troy* by the fact that it is a direct and drastic abridgement of Lydgate's *Troy-Book* —the first genuine *dérimage* in English—with some reminiscence too, it has been suggested, of Chaucer's *Troilus and Criseyde*.[1] A fourth translation, the prose *Siege of Jerusalem* (c. 1470), comes closer to general late fifteenth-century practice in that it is a translation from a French source, though in this instance a rather old-fashioned one, the thirteenth-century *Bible en françois* of Roger d'Argenteuil.[2] Another version of *The Siege of Jerusalem*, of about the same date, is a condensation of the popular romance of *Titus and Vespasian*.[3] It is a good example of the advantages of prose over verse in conciseness and readability.

[1] C. David Benson, 'Chaucer's Influence on the Prose "Sege of Troy"', *Notes and Queries* 18 (1971), 127–30.

[2] Phyllis Moe, 'Cleveland Manuscript W q 091.92—C 468 and the Veronica Legend', *Bull. of the New York Public Library* 70 (1966), 459–70. The *Bible en françois* is also a source of the alliterative *Siege of Jerusalem*: see the same author's essay in *Medium Aevum* 39 (1970), 147–54.

[3] To be precise, of the exemplar of MSS B and M of *Titus*: see *The Siege of Jerusalem in Prose*, ed. A. Kurvinen, Mémoires de la Société Néophilologique de Helsinki, xxxiv (Helsinki, 1969), p. 27. This work does not appear in the revised *Manual*.

The prose version of *Ipomydon* (c. 1460), to move on to chivalric romance proper, is likewise a *dérimage* of a traditional English romance. It is an abridged version of the tail-rhyme *Ipomadoun*, and can be set beside the popularized couplet version of the same poem, already mentioned, as an example of identical storymaterials being reshaped in different ways by the different demands of a reading and a listening audience. A more notable example of the same phenomenon, and one which points more significantly forward to the translations of Malory and Caxton, is the prose *Merlin* (c. 1450–60), based on the French prose *Merlin* of the Vulgate cycle. There was already in circulation a short text of the original English verse redaction of this same French prose romance. The short text is a variant version of the first quarter of the English poem as it appeared in the Auchinleck MS with the title *Arthour and Merlin*; it survives in a number of manuscripts based on a copy affected by oral transmission, and it is evidently the version familiar in performance, curtailed to the needs of two hours and equipped with the familiar (and welcome) forms of *délayage*. It may be assumed that by the mid-fifteenth century there was an audience that wanted a version of the story more suitable for reading, more comprehensive in scope and without the distractions of a text designed for performance. This audience was partly that created by expanding literacy, but it was also absorbing many upper-class readers who would previously have read these romances in the original French. The prose of the English version is close in construction and diction to the French, and there are few ways in which it would compel admiration, but it is clearly superior for its purpose to the verse of *Arthour and Merlin* and superior from every point of view to Lovelich's *Merlin*.

The prose romance of *Melusine* comes from somewhat later in the century, and may even post-date the French printed text of 1478, but it provides further clear evidence of the inevitability of the movement towards prose. Derived from a somewhat different version of the story of the Lusignan family to that which is translated in the *Romans of Partenay*, it is clear and consistent where the poem is obscure and confused, and though it is itself only a close and efficient translation of the French it points the direction in which the future of fiction lies. A last example of the growth of prose romance in English, and one which certainly precedes Caxton, is *King Ponthus and the Fair Sidone*. The French prose original was written to honour the famous La Tour Laundry family of Anjou, probably to match what had been done for the neighbouring family of Lusignan, and the method used, since the family had no ancestry worth speaking of, was to appropriate to the putative ancestor of the family, Ponthus, the exploits of Horn from the famous romance of *Horn et Rimel*. The French prose *Ponthus* was one of the romances included in the handsome volume (now British Library MS Royal 15.E.vi) presented by John Talbot, earl of Shrewsbury, to Margaret of Anjou in 1452. Whether or not it was in the royal library that Sir William Hopton, treasurer to Edward IV, came across the romance,[1] it was certainly for his family that the only complete surviving text of the English translation was copied about 1465. It forms part of MS Digby 185, containing also a *Brut* and long didactic poems by Hoccleve, and we can take it that the manuscript was prepared for the use of the family at their country house at Swillington in Yorkshire. The nature of the manuscript suggests a classic type for the audience of prose romance, just as the romance itself, which is written in a business-like and idiomatic prose, provides indisputable evidence that the taste for courtly prose romance was well advanced and in a fair way to being satisfied some time before the advent of Caxton.

V

Caxton himself provides the answers to most of our remaining questions about the development of romance in the fifteenth century, but Caxton's achievement is anticipated by Malory, who provided him with his major publishing *coup* and his only significant literary 'discovery'. Malory had his predecessors, as we have

[1] For a discussion of the MS, see Margaret Kekewich, 'Edward IV, William Caxton, and Literary Patronage in Yorkist England', *Mod. Lang. Review* 66 (1971), 481–7. There is an analysis of its contents in the Introduction (pp. 16–26) to the edition of *Le Rommant de Guy de Warwik et de Herolt d'Ardenne* by D. J. Conlon, Univ. of N. Ca. Studies in the Romance Languages and Literatures, no. 102 (Chapel Hill, 1971).

seen, and his work on the Vulgate *Merlin* is different only in quality from the translation in the earlier prose *Merlin*. His superiority in quality stems from his independence of mind, and modern notions of 'originality' have obscured this independence, which is his mark as a writer even when he is apparently most dependent on his source-materials. It is an independence of mind that is manifested in three main ways: as an architect, in his attempt to restructure the form of French prose narrative; as a moralist, in his attempt to reconstitute the matter of his source as a living model of secular chivalry in its ideal operation; and as a prose stylist. Modern writers, especially Vinaver,[1] have spoken eloquently and convincingly of the architect and moralist, but the prose stylist remains elusive, and perhaps Malory's superiority in quality to the English prose *Merlin* can only be demonstrated by comparison of parallel passages:[2]

Whan thei were alle assembled, Arthur dide hem grete honoure, and to hem made grete ioye and grete feste; and for thei were so high astates and men of grete puyssaunce, he made hem riche presentes, and yaf hem grete yeftes and riche, as he that therof hadde hym wele perveied. Whanne these barons saugh the grete yeftes and the riche presentz that the kynge hadde hem yoven, thei heilde therof grete disdeyn, and seide a-monge hem-self, That grete foles were they, whan of soche oon as he was of so base lynage, sholde be kynge of so worthi a reame as is the reame of logres, and seide that thei wolde it no lenger suffre. And thanne thei refused the yeftes that the kynge hadde hem offred, and yoven, and dide hem wele to wite that thei heilde hym not for ther kynge ne lorde, but that he sholde in all haste voide oute of the londe and the contree, so that he were no more seyn ther-in; and yef he wolde not voide the londe, and thei myght hym take, they lete hym well to wite that ther was no more but he sholde be deed.

[1] Primarily in the Introduction to his 3-volume edition of *The Works of Sir Thomas Malory* (Oxford, 1947; 2nd ed., 1967). Vinaver's Commentary provides material for many of the following remarks.

[2] Prose *Merlin* (ed. EETS 10, 21, 36, 112), p. 108; Malory, *Works*, ed. cit., i. 17. This is the comparison suggested by R. W. Ackerman in his essay on 'English Rimed and Prose Romances' in *Arthurian Literature in the Middle Ages*, ed. R. S. Loomis (Oxford, 1959), p. 489.

And kyng Arthur was glad of their comynge, for he wende that al the kynges and knyghtes had come for grete love and to have done hym worship at his feste, wherfor the kyng made grete joye and sente the kynges and knyghtes grete presentes. But the kynges wold none receyve, but rebuked the messagers shamefully and said they had no joye to receyve no yeftes of a berdles boye that was come of lowe blood, and sente hym word they wold none of his yeftes, but that they were come to gyve hym yeftes with hard swerdys betwixt the neck and the sholders; and therfore they came thyder, so they told to the messagers playnly, for it was grete shame to all them to see suche a boye to have a rule of soo noble a reaume as this land was.

One might speak here of the sharp, colloquial and dramatic idiom of Malory as against the diffuse and colourless quality of the earlier translation. More broadly speaking, what Malory has done is to absorb the original by imaginative process and re-present it *as* English, rather than translate it *into* English. It is a skill Caxton never mastered, nor valued very much.[1]

Malory's originality is demonstrated in another very significant way in the whole conception and method of his work. Here it can be claimed that he anticipated by more than a decade, if his work was completed about 1469–70, Caxton's attempt to transplant Burgundian culture in England, and yet did so in a manner that was independent enough to rank as an original innovation. His treatment of the alliterative *Morte Arthure*, for instance, is a piece of *dérimage* for which previous work in English furnishes only a humble precedent but which finds a close parallel in contemporary Burgundian work on the *chansons de geste*. Like the Burgundian redactors, most of whom have an association with duke Philip or his household, Malory shows himself anxious to reduce the barbarism and ferocity of his original, especially in the description of battle-scenes; to reduce the number of monologues

---

[1] Caxton's practice of close translation is the usual one in the 15th century. The view of S. K. Workman (*Fifteenth Century Translation as an Influence on English Prose*, Princeton Studies in English, 18, 1940) is that a phase of close translation was essential to the development of a complex syntax in English prose. He does not deal with Malory, whose work he calls 'recension', not translation.

and dialogues and so create an air of more continuous objective narration; to add more precise geographical references; and to omit descriptions of scenery and all those forms of rhetorical elaboration that had become so much a part of the poet's art.[1] Malory later moves beyond *dérimage* in his use of the stanzaic *Le Morte Arthur*, an act of plunder which bespeaks the mature creative artist.

In larger terms, one might see Malory's whole enterprise as a parallel to the massive compilations of David Aubert and Jean Wauquelin. In Burgundy it was the age of the *recueil*, and the aim was to give the whole history of, say, Charlemagne or Guillaume d'Orange by assembling the scattered materials of the cycle and rewriting them in the fashionable prose of the age. Whatever arguments may be entertained concerning the ultimate 'unity' of his work, Malory clearly writes out of the same desire to be comprehensive, and with him too the patchwork often shows. In more detailed matters of treatment he also offers many parallels to the practice of Burgundian writers: like them, he subordinates the fabulous and supernatural elements in the stories and introduces a greater degree of verisimilitude, in geographical, social and other references; he interprets events in a more realistic and contemporaneous way; he stresses incidents and characters which are important to the continuity of the cycle as a whole; and he writes as if he believes in the historical veracity of the story.[2] His fervent belief in its importance is radically different from the fashionable gestures of Burgundian writers towards contemporary chivalry, though perhaps the tone of some of his comments on Arthurian and contemporary *moeurs* echoes the redactor of *Gui de Warwick*, who writes, when Guy shows signs of forgetting Felice,

> Et je ne m'en merveille pas, car au jour d'huy en voit on assez qui pour moins de chose brisent le festu.[3]

[1] For Malory, see Vinaver's Commentary, as cited above; for the French redactors, see Doutrepont, *Les Mises en Prose*, pp. 488, 569, 586, 591.

[2] For the French redactors, see Doutrepont, *Les Mises en Prose*, pp. 504, 533, 598, 600, 618.

[3] Quoted in Doutrepont, op. cit., p. 626.

All in all, and setting aside the difference in quality, it might not be too misleading a generalization to say that Malory did for Arthur and Lancelot what the Burgundian translators and compilers were doing for Charlemagne and his paladins.

VI

Caxton, of course, was intimately acquainted with Burgundian literary culture, and it was he who was principally responsible for shaping and satisfying the taste for romances of chivalry which dominated the last quarter of the century.[1] To a large extent he exercised this responsibility by translating into English the Burgundian romances and pseudo-historical compilations that he had become familiar with during his long sojourn on the continent. He began his printing activities at Bruges in 1473–4 with his translation of *The Recuyell of the Historyes of Troye*, and continued after the setting up of the Westminster press with *Jason* (1477), *Godefroy of Boloyne* (1481), *Charles the Grete* (1485), *Paris and Vienne* (1485), *Blanchardin and Eglantine* (1488), *The Four Sons of Aymon* (1489) and *Eneydos* (1490). Caxton's work in this field was one of pure transplantation. Burgundian literary culture was his model of what culture should be, and his translations are as close as the differences of English will permit, and sometimes closer.

Caxton's admiration for Burgundian literary fashion is nowhere more clearly demonstrated than in his adaptation of his copy for *Le Morte Darthur*. Malory was working, I have suggested, within the tradition of the Burgundian prose *recueil*, but what he had done was not enough for Caxton, who proceeded to tailor it still more closely to the Burgundian model. His desire to create more strongly the impression that this was 'the whole book' of Arthur led him to suppress Malory's rubrics and book-divisions, as they appear in the Winchester MS, and to superimpose his own, breaking the work into chapters which could more readily be conceived of as relating to a continuous history. What Gaston Paris says of the most prolific of the Burgundian compilers can be transferred without adaptation to Caxton:

[1] See N. F. Blake, 'William Caxton: his Choice of Texts', *Anglia* 83 (1965), 289–307; also the same author's *Caxton and his World* (London, 1969), pp. 64–78.

Les rubriques nous montrent que David Aubert a essayé de donner à la vie de son héros une unité qu'elle n'avait pas reçue jusque-là dans les récits fabuleux dont il était l'objet.[1]

Caxton's freedom with his English copy is quite different from his slavish adherence to his French originals, and is most striking in his adaptation of Malory's *Tale of King Arthur and the Emperor Lucius*.[2] Here he presses still further the modifications that Malory had made in his version of the alliterative poem, cutting down what was left of the battle-scenes, reducing the number of speeches allocated to minor characters, and allowing Arthur and Gawain to emerge more strongly, in conformity with the needs of 'the whole book', as chivalric exemplars. He shows his distaste, too, for what he elsewhere calls 'olde and homely termes'[3] by systematically suppressing the alliterative language that still survives in Malory's adaptation, bringing the book more into line with his own notions of courtly style.

The audience that Caxton was catering for was presumably a well-to-do one. He does his best, in his dedications, to suggest that he is working at the direct request of a whole series of royal and noble patrons, but Blake shows convincingly that these are a form of publisher's blurb, and suggest no more than that a 'patron' had agreed to be mentioned.[4] Caxton was a commercial bookseller, perhaps that above all, and he recognized that references to aristocratic patrons would appeal strongly to readers not of noble birth who would be made to feel that they were enjoying and profiting from works of literature hitherto restricted to the more privileged classes.[5] Yet in a sense Caxton was perfectly justified in fostering this impression, for, though Edward IV may have preferred to collect lavishly illustrated Flemish copies of the French originals,[6]

[1] Quoted in Doutrepont, op. cit., p. 65.

[2] See Blake, *Caxton and his World*, pp. 111, 183.

[3] In the Prologue to *Eneydos*, printed in *Caxton's Own Prose*, p. 79.

[4] Blake, *Caxton and his World*, pp. 64, 86–8, 95–9, 151, 159. See also H. S. Bennett, *English Books and Readers 1475–1557* (Cambridge, 1952; 2nd ed., 1969), pp. 10–18.

[5] See C. E. Pickford, 'Fiction and the Reading Public in the Fifteenth Century', *Bull. of the John Rylands Library* 45 (1962–3), 423–38 (p. 436).

[6] See the article by Kekewich cited above, page 75; also Caxton's comment in the Prologue to *Jason* that he does not presume to present the work to Edward

the originals themselves were those that Caxton was translating and publishing; this was not surprising, since both Edward IV and Caxton had their tastes formed in the same Burgundian environment. The only difference was the difference of language, and Caxton was obscuring this as well as he could. So there would be no reason to suggest that the audience of 'vertuouse yong noble gentylmen and wymmen' proposed for *Blanchardin*[1] is at all a figment of Caxton's imagination. But equally, there would be no reason to suppose that these romances did not appeal to the wealthy London burghers with a taste for self-improvement whose custom was so important for Caxton's business. Caxton's admiration for the high chivalric idealism of the past is as old-fashioned as Malory's, and it may seem that both of them are engaged in erecting 'a temple of absurdly towering proportions for the veneration of an already decadent ideal,'[2] but all the evidence is that their readers, middle and upper class alike, were happy to share in the act of veneration. Nevertheless, one is tempted to look in Caxton's translations for some sign of the influence of the wealthy bourgeois audience which must have provided him with many of his best customers, to detect some movement of taste in the direction of 'l'esprit bourgeois' such as Besch claims to find in the Burgundian romances.[3] Perhaps *Paris and Vienne* is the nearest to a 'new' kind of romance. Based on an original of southern French provenance, it is a story more circumstantial, local and realistic in detail than at all usual, and is introduced by the redactor of the original French prose version with some suggestive remarks about the old romances. He has always, he says, been fond of reading 'romans et croniques des ystoyres enciennes' such as those of Lancelot and Tristan, though 'pluseurs chouses y ay trouvees qui moult sont impossibles a croyre'. He

---

[1] *Caxton's Own Prose*, p. 57.

[2] Ferguson, *Indian Summer of English Chivalry*, p. 10.

[3] E. Besch, 'Les adaptations en prose des chansons de geste au XVe et au XVIe siècle', *Revue du Sezième Siècle* 3 (1915), 155–81. Cf. Margaret Schlauch, *Antecedents of the English Novel 1400–1600* (Warsaw and London, 1963), pp. 47–78.

IV 'for as moch I doubte not his good grace hath it in Frensh which he wele understandeth' (*Caxton's Own Prose*, p. 104).

has decided to translate the present story not only because it tells of the noble deeds of men of former times but also 'quar la matiere me semble estre bien raisonnable et asses creable, et aussi que l'ystoyre est asses plaisant.'[1] Caxton's translation is one of his best, and the verisimilitude of treatment characteristic of his original comes over effectively, particularly in the episode where Vienne and her mother go visiting (pp. 21–3) or another episode where the elopement of the lovers is thwarted by a river swollen with recent rains and they have to put up in a nearby church (p. 36). The simple and circumstantial merits of a romance like this are not in danger of being overpraised when they have to compete with the haunting and suggestive effect created by the laconic treatment and accidental collocations of traditional verse-romance, but we have the beginnings here, perhaps, of the more realistic spirit of sixteenth-century fiction and of the absorption of romance into forms of *novella*.

The remainder of this history belongs largely to the sixteenth century and can be briefly told. Caxton's work on the translation of the longer prose romances of chivalry was continued, partly by independent writers like the translator of the Burgundian *The Three Kings' Sons* (c. 1500),[2] but chiefly under the auspices of his successor at the Westminster press, Wynkyn de Worde, who commissioned translations of *Valentine and Orson* and *Olyver of Castille* from William Watson, as well as a new translation of *King Ponthus*. He also reprinted many of Caxton's translations. Robert Copland contributed a version of *Helyas, Knight of the Swan*, and this phase in the history of English romance may be said to have been completed with the translations by Lord Berners of *Huon of Bordeaux*, of *Arthur of Litell Brytayne* and of Froissart. Berners' interest in chivalry is a 'romantic' one, not a living and practical interest such as Malory and Caxton still retained. Long before this, de Worde had moved his press from Westminster to Fleet Street, and in so doing begun to bring books

[1] Caxton's *Paris and Vienne*, ed. M. Leach (EETS 234, 1957), p. xv.

[2] There are hints of 'l'esprit bourgeois' here, especially in the episode where the French prince stays at the house of a citizen in Toledo and teaches his daughters harping and chess 'and all such goodly thynges as bilonge to a gentil-woman of honour' (p. 10).

closer to the needs and pockets of the 'ordinary' reader. He lacked Caxton's contacts with the aristocracy and upper bourgeoisie, as well as Caxton's more personal taste for the luxury trade, and, like Pynson, he saw the future of commercial printing in the larger and less exclusive audience. As far as the romances were concerned, the effect of this was to bring back into favour the earlier verse-romances which were still circulating in manuscript and which Pynson and de Worde printed off from time to time in small quarto volumes for a few pence.[1] The trade was still brisk enough in mid-century for William Copland to put out a dozen or so of the old romances but by this time they were becoming a joke and were well on their way to their last resting-place in the chapbooks (though assured of resurrection, as medieval literature).

A survey of fifteenth-century romance is suggestive of several significant changes that were taking place in the nature of literature and its relation to its audience. A larger reading public was developing, partly because of expanding literacy and partly because of the annexation by English of roles formerly filled by French. This reading audience grew as the listening audience declined, and its tastes are reflected in the development of prose romance, particularly after the introduction of printing. At the same time one has to recognize a remarkable tenacity in the survival of the older forms of romance, evidenced in the persistent recopying and reprinting of the traditional verse-romances, and in the survival too of the traditional chivalric idealism of romance, which was given renewed life in the new forms. The changes are radical and far-reaching but the continuities are important: they are the means by which a particular view of medieval chivalry is transmitted to later ages and so becomes an integral part of the experience of history; and they give significant direction to the subsequent development of narrative fiction.

[1] Bennett, *English Books and Readers*, p. 149. For a specific study, see R. S. Crane, 'The Vogue of *Guy of Warwick* from the Close of the Middle Ages to the Romantic Revival', *PMLA* 30 (1915), 125–94.

V

About Troilus

E. G. STANLEY

IT IS my purpose to bolster up Troilus, the hero of Chaucer's poem, in the hope that he may be more sympathetically considered than, I think, he has been; and that we may try to remember him as perhaps he should be remembered.

Before or about the time that Chaucer wrote the *Troilus* he refers to its hero in *The Parliament of Fowls* (291)[1] in a list in which Criseyde cannot be mentioned, for it is a register of those immortalized in the temple of Venus. Her infidelity does not admit her to the company of saints and martyrs of Love. More significantly, Chaucer causes himself to be rebuked by the God of Love in the Prefaces to *The Legend of Good Women*. In the earlier version (332–5) Love accuses Chaucer of having made men distrust women as a result of his setting forth the example of Criseyde; there is no mention of Troilus. In the later version the subject of the book is 'How that Crisseyde Troilus forsok' (265); and the title of the book is twice given there in Alceste's charge as *Crisseyde* (344 and 431), and similarly once in the earlier version (441); never as *Troilus*. That in itself shows that Love and the ladies who attend upon him have got their order wrong as they accuse Chaucer.

In a minor poem, probably by Chaucer though the attribution is made without firm authority and the poem could be the work of an exceptionally successful imitator of Chaucer's rime royal, an unnamed lady is rebuked as deserving to be canonized for her *brotelnesse* 'Bet than Dalyda, Creseyde or Candace'.[2] The first of the three is Delilah, Samson's shrew; the last is probably Ovid's

---

[1] Chaucer is quoted throughout from F. N. Robinson's second edition, 1957, but his punctuation is not always adhered to. Line references are to this edition.

[2] Robinson, p. 540, line 16.

Canace (*Heroides* XI) of whom Chaucer speaks at greater length
in the introduction to the Man of Law's Tale (77–80):

> But certeinly no word ne writeth he
> Of thilke wikke ensample of Canacee,
> That loved hir owene brother synfully—
> Of swiche cursed stories I sey 'Fy!'

National disaster followed Samson's love for Delilah. The personal
tragedy brought about by the incestuous love of Macareus and
Canace is told by Ovid with passion. In all three stories, Delilah's,
Canace's and Criseyde's, love leads to disaster and destroys
innocence itself, Samson, the child born to Canace, and Troilus.

Chaucer sufficiently named his poem 'the book of Troilus' in
one of his sobrest and sombrest moments when at the end of *The
Canterbury Tales* he takes leave and revokes it as the first of his
retractions.[1] That some of his contemporaries too called it so is
borne out by Thomas Usk's use of the name 'the boke of Troylus'
in a part of his *Testament of Love* where Love praises Chaucer
as if in retraction of his words in Chaucer's *Legend of Good
Women*; Usk was writing in the 1380's—he was beheaded in
March 1388.[2] Lydgate, however, in the *Troy Book* gives the title
of Chaucer's poem as 'his boke of Troylus and Criseyde';[3] and he
uses the same title in an unambiguous, but presumably un-
authoritative statement about the name Chaucer himself gave the
work:

> And in our vulgar, longe or that he deide,
> Gaff it the name off Troilus & Cresseide.
>   (*Fall of Princes*, I, 286–7)[4]

Caxton's edition of *c.* 1483 has no title, but the explicit avoids
both the bare *Troilus* and Lydgate's title, calling Chaucer's poem
in a way that shows clearly the superior importance of Troilus to

---

[1] *Canterbury Tales*, x (I) 1085.
[2] W. W. Skeat, *Complete Works of Geoffrey Chaucer*, VII (1897), p. xx for the
date, p. 123 lines 258–9.
[3] III, 4199; ed. H. Bergen, EETS ES 103 (1908), p. 515.
[4] ed. H. Bergen, EETS ES 121 (1924), p. 8.

Criseyde: 'Here endeth Troylus as/touchyng Creseyde'. Wynkyn de Worde's explicit in the 1517 edition rhymes *heuy* 'tragic' with *deny*: 'Thus endeth the treatyse of Troylus the heuy/By Geffraye Chaucer'. With Richard Pynson in 1526 the modern title is established: 'Here begynneth the boke of Troylus and Creseyde / newly printed by a trewe copye'.[1]

Whatever the book is called, *Troilus* or *Troilus and Criseyde*, it is impossible to think of Troilus other than as Criseyde's true lover. It is right that we should see their story from Troilus' side: for he stands for truth in love and she for falsehood. 'I have been false, light and foolish,' says Briseida in Benoit de Sainte Maure's *Roman de Troie*,[2] speaking of her love of Troilus and vowing to do better in her new love of Diomedes. Boccaccio's formulation at the end of *Il Filostrato* rings the changes on the wider theme of 'Frailty, thy name is woman' with special application to the tale of Criseida:

> O young men in whom amorous desire rises with the years, I beg you in God's name that you restrain the ready strides to that fierce appetite and see yourselves mirrored in the love of Troiolo that my poem now has set before you, because if you read it with mind and heart you will not lightly trust all ladies.
>
> A young lady is fickle and wishes for many lovers. She prizes her beauty more highly than accords with her looking-glass. She has the triumphant vainglory of her youth which is to her more pleasing and enchanting the more she herself appraises it. She has no sense of virtue or understanding, at all times fluttering as a leaf in the wind.[3]

[1] Cf. C. F. E. Spurgeon, *Five Hundred Years of Chaucer Criticism and Allusion*, I, Chaucer Society, 2nd Series 48, (1914) pp. 60, 72, 75. The British Library copy [C. 132. i. 38] of the 1517 edition has a laid-down title-page with *The noble and amerous aŭcyent hystory of Troylus and Cresyde / in the tyme of the Syege of Troye.*

[2] Line 20249; ed. L. Constans, SATF, III (1907), p. 291.

[3] VIII. 29–30. I have used the text of V. Branca's edition of *Il Filostrato*, in *Tutte le Opere di G. Boccaccio*, II (Milan, 1964); references are to parts and stanzas. The translation by N. E. Griffin and A. B. Myrick, *The Filostrato of G. Boccaccio*, Philadelphia 1929, has been consulted, and use has been made of W. M. Rossetti, *Chaucer's Troylus and Criseyde compared with Boccaccio's Filostrato*, Chaucer Society, 2nd Series 9 (1873).

Robert Henryson must have read a lesson not unlike that out of
Chaucer's *Troilus* when he leads Cresseid to punishment, and in
'The Complaint of Cresseid' at the end of *The Testament of
Cresseid*[1] to self-execration:

> Thy lufe, thy lawtie, and thy gentilnes
> I countit small in my prosperitie,
> Sa efflated I was in wantones,
> And clam upon the fickill quheill sa hie.
> All faith and lufe I promissit to the,
> Was in the self fickill and friuolous:
> O fals Cresseid, and trew knicht Troilus!

In his adaptation of Shakespeare's *Troilus and Cressida*, Dryden
rescues her from such shame and degradation, making his Troilus
say (in the middle of the double suicide scene to which Dryden's
sense of poetical justice leads):[2]

> But oh, thou purest, whitest innocence,—
> For such I know thee now, too late I know it!

Since, however, Dryden had to abandon the *donnée* of the
famous story and stand it on its head to achieve his ending it is
best to go no further in the development of the story in English
literature than Shakespeare's scene of protestations and prophecy,
which arising, as it does, out of the vows in Chaucer's poem,[3]
provides the summing up given, by the most literary reader to
have studied it, to three of the characters in Chaucer's poem:[4]

> *Cressida.*   for to be wise and loue
>   Exceeds mans might: that dwels with gods aboue.
> *Troylus.* O that I thought it could be in a woman—

[1] 547–53; ed. D. Fox(London, 1968), p. 81.
[2] v.ii; ed. Sir W. Scott, *Works of J. Dryden*, 2nd edn. (Edinburgh, 1821), VI,
p. 360.
[3] III.1492–8, and especially IV.1528–1659. Cf. R. K. Presson, *Shakespeare's*
Troilus and Cressida & *the Legends of Troy* (Madison, 1953), pp. 119–20.
[4] III.ii.157–99. I quote the text of F_1 from the New Variorum Edition, ed. H.
N. Hillebrand (Philadelphia, 1953), pp. 158–63, with some changes.

As, if it can, I will presume in you—
To feede for aye her lampe and flames of loue,
To keepe her constancie in plight and youth,
Out-liuing beauties outward, with a minde
That doth renew swifter then blood decaies;
Or that perswasion could but thus conuince me
That my integritie and truth to you
Might be affronted with the match and waight
Of such a winnowed puritie in loue.
How were I then vp-lifted! but alas,
I am as true as truths simplicitie
And simpler then the infancie of truth.

Cressida. In that I'le warre with you.

Troylus.   O vertuous fight.
When right with right wars, who shall be most right?
True swaines in loue shall in the world to come
Approue their truths by *Troylus*: when their rimes,
Full of protest, of oath and big compare,
Wants similes—truth tir'd with iteration,
As true as steele, as plantage to the Moone,
As Sunne to day, as Turtle to her mate,
As Iron to Adamant, as Earth to th'Center—
Yet after all comparisons of truth
As truths authenticke author to be cited:
As true as *Troylus* shall crowne vp the Verse,
And sanctifie the numbers.

Cressida.   Prophet may you be:
If I be false or swerue a haire from truth,
When time is old and hath forgot it selfe,
When water drops haue worne the Stones of *Troy*
And blinde obliuion swallow'd Cities vp,
And mightie States characterlesse are grated
To dustie nothing, yet let memory
From false to false, among false Maids in loue,
Vpbraid my falsehood: when they'aue said as false
As Aire, as Water, as Winde, as sandie earth,
As Foxe to Lambe, as Wolfe to Heifers Calfe,
Pard to the Hinde, or Stepdame to her Sonne,
Yea, let them say, to sticke the heart of falsehood,
As false as *Cressid*.

There is no need to quote the Pandar's protestation, in prose, in which he prophesies that 'all brokers betweene' shall be named after him, for the prophecy is made after the event: *pander* was established as a common noun to describe a practitioner of the craft of pimping early in the sixteenth century—though it can be said that that is itself a nation's judgement on the character in Chaucer's poem.

The accusation that Pandarus is a pander goes back to his inventor, Boccaccio.[1] Twice, fairly early in *Il Filostrato*, Pandaro accuses himself. At III.6 he says to Troiolo, 'For you I have become a *mezzano*, for you I have thrown my honour to the ground, for you I have corrupted the pure breast of *mia sorella* [i.e. his cousin Criseida] and put your love in her heart.' There is no need to attach credence to Pandaro's profession of faith in Criseida's *petto sano*; but the word *mezzano* sticks: it may be translated anywhere in the semantic scale that leads from 'middle-man' to 'pimp'.

Fame has proclaimed Cressida throughout the later Middle Ages and thereafter as one who was false, because she gave pleasure to two princes rather than content to one. In *Il Filostrato* (III.8) Pandaro expresses his concern for his cousin's reputation, telling Troiolo that he has Criseida's reputation in his power, and that if she loses it through Troiolo's failure to preserve their love secret shame will fall on Pandaro too 'who am at the same time her kinsman and her *trattator*', a word which appears to have the same range of meanings as *mezzano* but was rarer. Chaucer (III.250–73) is less direct than Boccaccio. He understands *mezzano* correctly, but appears to misunderstand *trattator* and translates it 'traitour'.[2] In both Boccaccio and Chaucer, Troiolo's forceful rejection of that self-accusation—'do not use that base name to describe yourself' (*Il Filostrato* III.16)—leads to that ultimate proof of equality in manly friendship, Troiolo's offer to Pandaro of his young sister Polyxena, most highly prized for beauty, or of his loveliest

---

[1] Benoit de Sainte Maure has the name Pandarus for a quite unconnected king of Sezile, an ally of Priam's. See edn. Constans, v (1909), p. 71, s.n.

[2] See W. M. Rossetti, op. cit., p. 115. The error could well be mediate between Boccaccio and Chaucer.

kinswoman Helen. Troiolo, to prove that such things are honest to do for a friend, offers unasked to Pandaro what Pandaro is in the process of doing for Troiolo. Chaucer follows Boccaccio:

> And, that thow knowe I thynke nought ne wene
> That this servise a shame be or jape,
> I have my faire suster Polixene,
> Cassandre, Eleyne, or any of the frape,
> Be she nevere so fair or wel yshape,
> Telle me which thow wilt of everychone
> To han for thyn ...   (III.407–13)

There is in Chaucer's wording a significantly lower tone in speaking of the ladies of the House of Troy than in Boccaccio's. Furthermore, it is difficult to envisage Cassandra as Pandarus' partner. In the context of the true and loyal friendship of Troiolo and Pandaro as presented to us by Boccaccio I am ready to defend Troiolo's offer; but it saddens me in Chaucer. The reason for this difference lies in the change Chaucer has made from Pandaro to Pandarus. I see no change from Troiolo to Troilus, except to the extent to which he is touched by the lowering in the value of Pandarus.

It has often been remarked that Boccaccio's two young men, Troiolo and Pandaro, are honest friends. The first words about Pandaro are that he is 'a Trojan youth of high lineage and full of spirit' (*molto coraggioso*. II.1). At every stage it is made clear that there is loyal friendship between them. They address each other in terms of dear friendship, and Pandaro's statement early in the poem (II.5) that it is right for a man to share everything with his friend, sorrow and joy, shapes their actions nobly to the bitter end. When Troiolo dreamt how a savage boar, identified on awakening with Diomede, has torn out Criseida's heart with his snout—and she almost enjoyed it—Pandaro restrains his friend from suicide (VII.24–36), urging him rather to fight the Greeks, both of them together, and in that battle as youths of honour to die like men in slaying enemies (VII.45). We are not told if, in fact, when Troiolo was killed Pandaro was out fighting Greeks by Troiolo's side: perhaps Pandaro is not of sufficient consequence for us to wish to know, perhaps Boccaccio assigns to him no other activity than that of a go-between, leading his cousin to his friend, and when they are apart carrying messages for Troiolo even into the Greek camp (vɪɪɪ.3). Be that as it may; the words of loving friendship between them (e.g. ɪɪɪ.13–14) and of honest speech when Pandaro tries to inspirit Troiolo and make him abate the excesses of sorrow after Criseida's departure (v.31), bluntly calling him a *misorno* (which appears to mean something like 'poor fish') and accusing him (v.35) of behaving foolishly and strangely, seem evidence of something nobler than a hanger-on of a prince.

There can be no equality between a prince of the House of Troy and a youth of that city, though well-born, and that not merely because of the difference in rank between royalty and nobility. The princes of Troy have a special place in the foundation myths of both Italy and Britain, believed in as fact in English medieval and Renaissance historiography, as readers of Geoffrey of Monmouth, of *Sir Gawain and the Green Knight*, and, in modern works, of the first book of Milton's *History of Britain* know.[1] The Trojan Aeneas and his descendants founded cities and states in Latium, Tuscany, Lombardy, Sicily, France, and, far to the west through Brutus, Britain, so that a special piety encompasses the princes of Troy.

Hector, Priam's eldest son, is the most glorious as the first of the Nine Worthies, and Troilus, Priam's fifth and last legitimate son,[2] shares in the veneration felt for the five sons of Priam. The second son, Paris, caused the Trojan Wars by the Rape of Helen, and so bears blame for the slaughter and dispersal of the first great court of chivalry. His infamy is increased by his killing the unarmed Achilles in a shameful ambush.[3] The third of the brothers, Dei-

[1] See E. Faral, *La Légende Arthurienne* (Paris, 1929), ɪ, pp. 170–82; J. S. P. Tatlock, *Legendary History of Britain* (Berkeley and Los Angeles, 1950); Sir T. D. Kendrick, *British Antiquity* (London, 1950); George Gordon, 'The Trojans in Britain', *Essays and Studies*, ɪx (1923), reprinted in his *The Discipline of Letters* (Oxford, 1923); H. Matter, *Englische Gründungssagen. . .* , Anglistische Forschungen, 58, 1922.

[2] See Benoit, line 2943, ed. Constans, ɪ (1904), p. 149; Guido delle Colonne *Historia Destructionis Troiae*, v, ed. N. E. Griffin (Cambridge Mass), 1936), p. 44.

[3] Benoit, lines 21838–22334; ed. Constans, ɪɪɪ, pp. 373–99. Guido, xxvɪɪ; ed. Griffin, p. 207.

phebus, is honourable, and, in Boccaccio's account followed by
Chaucer, he is closest to Troilus;[1] according to Benoit he is
eventually killed in the Wars and greatly lamented.[2] The fourth
of the brothers, Helenus, is the least important; neither Boccaccio
nor Chaucer mentions him.

Inevitably, therefore, Troilus is enhanced by association with
Trojan chivalric story.[3] The highest praise he can be given is
'Troilus, / The wise, worthi Ector the secounde' (II.157–8)—
spoken, however, by the untrustworthy Pandarus when he is
trying to interest his niece in the young man:

> Tyl she gan axen hym how Ector ferde,
> That was the townes wal and Grekes yerde.

> 'Ful wel, I thonk it God,' quod Pandarus,
> 'Save in his arm he hath a litel wownde;
> And ek his fresshe brother Troilus,
> The wise, worthi Ector the secounde,
> In whom that alle vertu list habounde,
> As alle trouth and alle gentilesse,
> Wisdom, honour, fredom, and worthinesse.'
>   (II.153–161)

The beginning of that exchange, Criseyde's prattle and her
uncle's chitchat, are part of the characterization of the two, but
what follows, the last four lines, rise above that, and are part of
Chaucer's art of poetic discourse and too high to be attributable to
his art of characterization of speakers which is subordinated to it.

Troilus cannot be taken away from his Trojan background, in
which he played a prominent part. At the same time, the other
members of the royal House of Troy are too famous to allow of

---

[1] *Il Filostrato*, VII.77; *Troilus*, II.1408–11.

[2] Lines 19099–140; ed. Constans, III, pp. 229–31.

[3] It might be thought that special honour would have accrued to Troilus
because of his etymological connection with Troy; but there is no evidence of
that in Boccaccio or Chaucer. In later English verse something of the kind may
be seen in the sixteenth-century *Court of Love*, line 872, 'Troilus, Troyes knight',
without any elaboration [Skeat, *Works of Chaucer*, VII, p. 432—with an unneces-
sary emendation].

their relegation to mere attendants on Troilus, the youngest of
them, in his private joys and griefs of love: Priam and Hecuba,
Hector and Andromache, Paris and Helen, and brother-in-law
Aeneas hold the stage when they enter. It is instructive to see how
Boccaccio (often followed by Chaucer) introduces Hector. In
three stanzas near the beginning Criseida appeals to Hector to
save her from popular anger at her father's defection, and he is
seen to have the power to grant the protection she seeks.[1] A little
later[2] we see the prominent part played by Hector and his brothers
in battle, and battle with Hector conspicuous in it is described
again in the opening stanzas of Part IV;[3] in words not followed
closely by Chaucer we learn how Hector's single valour could not
hold back the many Greeks, and Hector was in command of the
Trojan forces. Unlike Chaucer's account (IV.176–82), Boccaccio's
allows no part to Hector in the exchange of Criseyde for Antenor;
but he was present, for when Troiolo swoons at the decision
Hector was there to raise him up (IV.19). A little later (IV.31–2)
Boccaccio uses Troiolo's disregard of Trojan values to indicate
that Troiolo's grief has led him to go too far in his anguished
complaint to Fortune:

If my happy and favoured life displeased you, why did you
not lay low the glorious pride of Ilium? Why did you not take
from me my father, why not Hector on whose excellence rests
every hope in these sad times? Why did you not bear off
Polyxena, why not Paris and Helen too? If only Criseida were
left to me I should not care about any other great loss, nor utter
a word.[4]

In the dialogue between Diomede and Criseida Hector is men-
tioned twice,[5] once by him (VI.17) 'And if there were a dozen
Hectors as there is only one', and once by her (VI.28), that the
Trojans reveal their qualities 'in the hand of Hector'.

In Il Filostrato (and similarly in Chaucer) the youngest brother

[1] I.12–14; cf. Troilus, I.106–26.
[2] I.45; cf. Troilus, I.470–6.
[3] Troilus, IV.29–35.
[4] Cf. Troilus, IV.274–82.
[5] Neither mention is taken over by Chaucer, though he follows this part of
Il Filostrato (cf. IV.890–6, 967–73).

is overshadowed by Hector when it comes to affairs of state or the conduct of war; he is above Troiolo's reach as a confidant, and yet a man in love needs a confidant. In inventing Pandaro Boccaccio achieves two things: he shifts the centre of Trojan interest away from the valiant death of Hector or the Rape of Helen to the tragic love of Troiolo, and he provides Troiolo with a friend who does not detract from Troiolo by being of greater consequence than he. As has often been said, Pandaro combines being Troiolo's friend with having the *entrée* to Criseida: indeed, not only is the idea of that friendship emphasized throughout the poem, as we have seen, but a reference to Pandaro's irresistible powers of gaining admittance to Criseida in Boccaccio's account is memorable because it contains at least a germ, I think, of that familiarity between Pandarus and his niece Criseyde half-laughingly, half-sniggeringly described by Chaucer. Pandaro enters his cousin Criseida's room where she was uttering her cruel complaint on having to leave Troy: 'Pandaro came, for whom nobody was able to keep the door shut' (IV.95). It seems almost a hint, rare in Boccaccio, of insufficient breeding in Pandaro to be truly the prince's friend.

Cressida and her father Calchas seem to have no share in the high lineage of Pandarus. In none of the treatments of the story are we left in any doubt about the difference in rank between Troilus and Cressida. In Chaucer, he is royal but she only a scientist's daughter (I.67). Guide delle Colonne calls Calchas an *antistes*,[1] which we may translate 'chief priest' if we are thinking in Trojan terms or 'bishop' if we are thinking in medieval terms— Lydgate, for example, calls Calchas 'bishop'.[2] The difference in rank between Troilus and Cressida is in no other handling of the story as pronounced as in *Il Filostrato*. There appears to be no evidence that Boccaccio used Guido, and he may, therefore, not have regarded Calchas as anything other than a mere priest. The gulf in rank between Troiolo and Criseida seems much greater than the difference between Troiolo and Pandaro—and there is no explicit mention in the various treatments of the story of Troilus

[1] x; ed. Griffin, p. 98.
[2] *Troy Book*, II, 5977 f.; ed. Bergen, EETS ES 97 (1906), p. 315.

and Cressida that Pandarus and Calchas are related and therefore of equal rank. In Boccaccio's summing up of the story near the end (VIII.28) the love between Troiolo and 'the base Criseida' is described as misconceived. Cassandra, whose voice is that of truth in Trojan story, puts the matter with force: a great king's son 'in love, not with a noble lady, but with the daughter of an evil priest, a man who has lived badly and who does not matter' (VII.87). At this point, Troiolo's reply to his sister's clear-sighted view of things, his half-denial that he loves Criseida and his magniloquent 'Nobility is wherever virtue is' (VII.94) cannot efface the recollection of how pleased he was early in their amours (III.3) that in her letter to him (II.121) she humbly commends herself to his high honour, calling herself 'of little worth' (127). And when at last they met, her language is that of abject apology for having kept the prince's royal person waiting in some downstairs cubbyhole in her house (III.28): 'My Lord, if I have offended in keeping Your Royal Highness [*il tuo splendor reale*] shut in such a place, I pray by Heaven that you forgive me, O my sweet desire', and only the last phrase reveals a relationship other than that of inferiority of estate.[1] Chaucer reduces the difference in rank between the lovers; his Calkas is a lord (1.65), his Criseyde has a palace (II.76) and a considerable establishment. There is no discernible difference in rank between Chaucer's Criseyde and her uncle.

As has always been said, Chaucer's conception of Pandarus differs from Boccaccio's Pandaro. Pandarus is less straightforward, less to be trusted, more willing to say what he thinks Troilus would like to hear. In short, he is not so much Horatio to Troilus, but rather Rosencrantz and Guildenstern. Troilus is the least changed of the characters in Chaucer's adaptation of Boccaccio's story: if anything, he is less to be blamed, more to be pitied. Troiolo's timidity is mentioned explicitly by Boccaccio, both early (II.93) 'a timid lover', and later (IV.16) when, after the exchange of Criseida for Antenor is announced, Troiolo fails utterly in resolve. His timidity is carried over into Chaucer's account, and is increased in the process, so that it needs a more forceful Pandarus to

[1] Cf. K. Young, *The Origin and Development of the Story of Troilus and Criseyde*, Chaucer Society, 2nd Series 40 (1908), pp. 71–5.

get the lovers to bed together. Pandarus is also coarser, especially in his relationship with his niece Criseyde, coarser than Pandaro ever was with his cousin Criseida. Pandaro is of an age with Troiolo; but Pandarus seems older than Troilus. The hint early in *Il Filostrato* that Troiolo looked upon Pandaro as his wise friend— '*Tu savio, tu amico*' (II. 33)[1]—is turned by Chaucer into worldly wisdom, and as the story draws to its tragic close the hollowness of Pandarus as a friend becomes increasingly apparent as his courtier's skill in saying or doing nothing out of tune with his prince's mood of the moment comes to the fore, especially in the alternation of Troilus' hopes and fears as he waits for Criseyde's return. The element of the courtier is clearest perhaps in the excuses made by the narrator for Pandarus' absence from Troilus when he has most need of him in his lonely anguish:

> This Pandare, that of al the day biforn
> Ne myghte han comen Troilus to se—
> Although he on his hed it hadde sworn—
> For with the Kyng Priam alday was he,
> So that it lay nought in his libertee
> Nowher to gon. But on the morwe he wente
> To Troilus whan that he for hym sente.
>   (V.281–7)

By turning Pandarus into Criseyde's uncle Chaucer has not merely made one man at once confidant of the lover and guardian of the beloved, but he has turned a young coeval friend into an older, worldly-wise courtier in whom no prince should put his trust. Boccaccio had removed most of the historically important Trojan world from the love story; as a result of Chaucer's change in Pandarus he has put back, not the history as do the heavy-handed Lydgate and, with lighter touch, Shakespeare, but the ambience of a court. He has to that extent made the circumstances of the love-story more real. In the fourteenth century and later, for as long as princes of the blood had either influence and power, or at least hopes of influence and power, there was no young prince without an *entourage* of flattering courtiers out to establish

[1] Cf. *Troilus*, I.1052.

themselves in royal favour by pretending to solicitude for the
welfare of their patron. A favourite is a false friend: the role of
Horatio cannot be combined with that of a Rosencrantz or
Guildenstern. A prince may count himself fortunate if he has one
friend: it is inevitable that he should be surrounded by courtiers
pretending to be his friends and not easily distinguished from true
friends by an inexperienced prince. Experience will come to him
in adversity: 'A friend in need is a friend indeed' is a proverb not
included in the proverb-spouting Pandarus' repertoire.[1]

The role of courtier becomes more evident in Pandarus in the
last two books of the *Troilus*, as the face of friendship recedes in
adversity; but there are hints earlier. That combination of ver-
bosity and humour which Chaucer gives to Pandarus serves as a
shield preventing an answer to the questions, Is he sincere or is he
insincere?; and, How deep in Pandarus lie the emotions and the
thoughts that show themselves in tears and sobs, and merry
banter? Early it appears that Pandarus does not view his relationship with Troilus other than as that of an attendant upon a
gracious man of high rank, when he lays before his niece the merits
of Troilus so that she may take pity on him:

> Therto he is the friendlieste man
> Of gret estat that evere I saugh my lyve,
> And wher hym lest, best felawshipe kan
> To swich as hym thynketh able for to thryve.
>   (II.204–7)

['Moreover he is the friendliest man of high rank whom I have
seen in my life, and, where it pleases him, he is excellent company
with anyone who seems to him deserving to prosper.']

Taken over from Boccaccio is Pandarus' wish to entertain and
divert Troilus, most strikingly to while away the ten days between

---

[1] See *Canterbury Tales*, VII.1305–6 (B² 2495–6), where Chaucer (following his
source) ascribes it to Cato; but see Proverbs xvii.17. Cf. S. Singer, *Sprichwörter
des Mittelalters*, III (Bern, 1947), pp. 53–4; B. J. Whiting *Proverbs, Sentences . . .
before 1500* (Cambridge (Mass.), 1968), F634; B. J. Whiting, *Chaucer's Use of
Proverbs*, Harvard Studies in Comp. Lit., xi (1934), 120.

I should perhaps acknowledge that Rosencrantz and Guildenstern are seen as
in Goethe's *Wilhelm Meisters Lehrjahre*, v, v.

Criseyde's exchange and her promised return, culminating in his wish to drag Troilus off to the festive court of Sarpedon.[1] Pandarus flatters Troilus without restraint; Chaucer translates Pandaro's statement in *Il Filostrato* that Troiolo is six times wiser than he into 'A thousand fold'.[2] Perhaps the most revealing of Pandarus' skills as a courtier is in his handling of Troilus' brothers in arranging protection for Criseyde. Deiphebus, we learn, had always been his lord and great friend, (II.1403), language used by Pandarus a little earlier to address Troilus, 'Lord and frend and brother dere' (II.1359); and then he begins to manipulate Deiphebus, whose reactions are frank and friendly, everything a prince's conduct should be, in marked contrast to the fawning language of Pandarus (II.1406–58). When the Trojan princes are assembled 'This Pandarus gan newe his tong affile' (II.1681), the word *affile*, 'make smooth as with a file', indicating the smoothness of the courtier's speech. None of that is in Boccaccio. And my next instance is not in Boccaccio either. When Pandarus has contrived to get Troilus into Criseyde's bedroom in her uncle's house, and Troilus kneels at her bedside, it is difficult to disentangle, in the emphasis placed by Pandarus on the prince's condescension in kneeling to her and Pandarus' bringing of a cushion for him to place his knee on, what of his words and actions Chaucer means us to attribute to Pandarus' habits as a courtier and what to his habits as a man endowed with a sense of humour:

> But Pandarus, that so wel koude feele
> In every thyng, to pleye anon bigan,
> And seyde, 'Nece, se how this lord kan knele!
> Now, for youre trouthe, se this gentil man!'[2]
> And with that word he for a quysshen ran,
> And seyde, 'Kneleth now, while that yow leste
> There God youre hertes brynge soone at reste!'
>   (III.960–6)

The effect of all these Chaucerian changes is to make Troilus seem more gullible than Troiolo. Troiolo had a friend in Pandaro; Troilus is played upon by an older courtier. That is why Troilus'

---

[1] v.431; cf. *Il Filostrato*, v.38–40.
[2] *Il Filostrato*, II.91; *Troilus*, II.1002 f.

offer of Polyxena, Helen or any of the *frape* to the coarser and older
Pandarus saddens me in Chaucer's account as it does not in Boccaccio's. For a brief time in Book III it looks almost as if in
Chaucer's poem—Boccaccio has nothing to correspond with this
part—Troilus and Criseyde might allow their love to go no further
than friendship;[1] Troilus even finds the strength in him to be
absent from Criseyde and has Pandarus carrying letters between
them (III.488), an idea perhaps taken from a point in *Il Filostrato*
(II.21). Chaucer makes it seem that Pandarus manipulates the
characters and the situation so that they go beyond friendship;
but clearly he would not have succeeded in manipulating Troilus
and Criseyde to come together if they had had no wish for it—
and, more important, it is part of the *donnée* of the story and
cannot be altered without making nonsense of the rest.

Chaucer makes his Troilus appear younger not merely than
Pandarus but also than Criseyde. The levels of the generations
relative to each other is different in Boccaccio's Troy from
Chaucer's Troy, and that is always commented on in connection
with the change from Pandaro cousin to Criseida to Pandarus
uncle to Criseyde. At the same time as Chaucer makes that change
in their relative ages he introduces points to make Criseyde older.
She herself early in the poem insists on her being a maturer widow
more fit for the reading of saints' lives than for dancing:

> Quod Pandarus, '... ... ...
> Do wey youre barbe and shewe youre face bare!
> Do wey youre book, rys up, and lat us daunce,
> And lat us don to May som observaunce!'
>
> 'I? God forbede!' quod she, 'be ye mad?
> Is that a widewes lif, so God yow save?
> By God, ye maken me ryght soore adrad.
> Ye ben so wylde, it semeth as ye rave.
> It sate me wel bet ay in a cave
> To bidde and rede on holy seyntes lyves.
> Lat maydens gon to daunce, and yonge wyves!'
>
> (II.110–19)

[1] See especially III.451–510.

That she herself has nieces staying under her guidance in her palace invests her with an authority that, whenever Chaucer, their inventor, brings them in, makes her seem an older, responsible widow. Her uncertain age lies at the centre of the famous Chaucerian bathos at the end of her portrait late in the poem, 'But trewely, I kan nat telle hir age' (v.826), which makes me suspect that she is the wrong side of whatever age it was best to be the right side of in the fourteenth century.¹ I know the arguments in favour of a young Criseyde, that little girls were married as soon as they could be coaxed into babbling the responses in the marriage service, and how it is possible and a frequent occurrence to have an uncle no older than oneself or nieces no younger than oneself. It is, however, not likely that Chaucer would have introduced his major changes affecting the levels of the generations if he had not meant Pandarus to be older than his niece Criseyde and Criseyde older than her nieces of whom Antigone seems old enough to sing feelingly of love (II.824–96). As a result of these changes Troilus appears doubly younger than Troiolo. Youth and inexperience in love go together; Troilus has only just ceased to be a scorner of love. It would be wrong to think Criseyde is a Wife of Bath, except to whatever extent we may wish to apply to Criseyde the emphasis in the Wife of Bath on experience; experience goes with widowhood.²

Shakespeare implies the youth of Troilus in his protestation

> I am as true as truths simplicitie
> And simpler than the infancie of truth.
> (*Troilus and Cressida* III.ii.170–1)³

¹ Cf. E. G. Stanley, 'Stanza and Ictus: Chaucer's Emphasis in "Troilus and Criseyde"', in *Chaucer und seine Zeit: Symposion für Walter F. Schirmer*, ed. A. Esch, Buchreihe der Anglia 14 (1968), p. 130.

² *Canterbury Tales*, III (D) 1–3.

³ Cf. I.i.7–12, ed. Hillebrand, p. 8:

Troilus. The Greeks are strong & skilful to their strength,
   Fierce to their skill, and to their fiercenesse Valiant;
   But I am weaker then a womans teare,
   Tamer then sleepe, fonder then ignorance,
   Less valiant then the Virgin in the night,
   And skillesse as vnpractis'd Infancie.

The valour of Troilus in the Wars makes it unlikely, however, that he was only just halfway through his teens. Shakespeare gives him an authoritative voice in Trojan affairs, though elsewhere he contrasts Greek strength and skill with Troilus' being 'skillesse as vnpractis'd infancie'.[1] In the second scene of the play Pandarus, speaking to Cressida of Troilus, says 'O admirable youth! he ne're saw three and twenty'.[2] In the same scene there is much laughter at the small growth of beard on Troilus' chin.[3] Shakespeare seems to have advanced Troilus' age to under twenty-three because he (like Lydgate before him, though in a very different literary form) puts back a great deal of Guido's historical matter enriched by the love story which Shakespeare (but not Lydgate or Caxton in the *Recuyell of the Histories of Troye*)[4] makes the centre. In a world in which Troilus has a major political and military role to play he is not likely to have been a precocious teen-ager; and yet just under twenty-three seems older than my impression of Troilus even in Shakespeare's account. Perhaps that is why Dryden, in a part of his play in which he keeps much of Shakespeare, reduces the age to 'he never saw two-and-twenty';[5] but even that seems too old for Chaucer's Troilus. Shakespeare[6] and Dryden further[7] make Troilus active in his youthful way. Boccaccio and Chaucer make him languish more, and since they give him little part to play in affairs of state they also make him seem less competent.

Chaucer's own touch at the beginning is to have Troilus a scorner of love, and that adds to the general effect of his youth. He is not merely himself uninterested in love, but acts as the leader of a band of young knights whose pastime it is to gaze at ladies, praising them or dispraising them without involving themselves with them further (1.183–203). This scorning of love

---

[1] See fn. 3, opposite.
[2] I.ii.237–8; ed. Hillebrand, p. 34.
[3] I.ii.111–67; ed. Hillebrand, pp. 26–30.
[4] See Presson, op. cit., p. 3.
[5] I.ii.; ed. Scott, p. 280.
[6] Especially II.ii.26–98, ed. Hillebrand, pp. 95–102; and IV.v.306–23, ed. Hillebrand, pp. 252–3, where Troilus goes to the Greek camp.
[7] III.ii; ed. Scott, pp. 315–23.

leads to Troilus later feeling penitent, with the Pandar acting as his
confessor (1.932–8). In short, he scorned what he was too young
to have experienced. By the time Pandarus makes his first entrance
(1.548) Troilus has undergone so many contrary emotions and
expressed so many contradictory thoughts that, before we are
told about his martial valour, we have formed a lasting impression
of him as immature. Boccaccio is almost completely responsible
for that, because he removed Troiolo's love story from the Troy
of the Greek Wars by the effective device of giving him Pandaro
as a confidant who has no role to play in Trojan business of state;
and Chaucer heightens the effect of Troilus' immaturity by
making him scorn love till he himself is smitten by love.

But it is not just his youth and want of experience that make
Troilus seem a poor fish. He has swallowed too much of Guillaume's
teaching in the *Roman de la Rose*, is so anxious about preserving
Criseyde's reputation, and has been so ennobled by love that he
has had any rashness of youth knocked out of him, as he finds that
virtue in love cannot be reconciled with action. As we have seen,
Shakespeare to make Troilus more interesting puts in some
action, and as a result our hero is once again part of the glorious
history of Troy from which he was separated by Boccaccio.
Shakespeare's Prologue opens with the words 'In Troy there lyes
the Scene', and continues in language redolent of antique glory.
The first scene, after a little over a hundred lines of Troilus and
Pandarus, has an alarum and 'Enter Aeneas', no less, with 'How
now Prince *Troylus*? / Wherefore not a-field?' (1.i.110–12), and
Troilus with a manly jest about the wounded Paris:

> Let *Paris* bleed, 'tis but a fear to scorne:
> *Paris* is gor'd with *Menelaus* horne.
> (1.i.119–20)

In these words is a taste of that martial vigour that Chaucer alludes
to as manifesting itself in deeds. This is part of the missing side
of Troilus' fame as 'Ector the secounde'; Shakespeare has set up
the opposition, implicit in Chaucer's account, of courage in war
and timidity in love. Dryden, adapting the scene between Æneas
and Troilus, makes that opposition explicit:

Æneas.   Hark what good sport   [*Alarm within.*
Is out of town to-day! When I hear such music
I cannot hold from dancing.
Troilus.   I'll make one,
And try to lose an anxious thought or two
In heat of action.
Thus, coward-like, from love to war I run,
Seek the less dangers and the greater shun.[1]

Chaucer goes furthest in presenting the timidity Troilus shows in love. In *Il Filostrato* Criseida meets Troiolo before they go up to her chamber together. There it is she, not he, who feels, or acts as if she feels, some remnants of modesty as she is in bed together with Troiolo, and draws attention to the shift she has kept on, and it is he who asks her to remove it (III.31–2). In Chaucer's telling such boldness in love is not shown by Troilus; it has been sacrificed to a more pandering Pandarus and to the humour of the situation: Troilus, inactive even at this stage because he feels so guilty to have caused Criseyde's tears (III.1065–89) that he swoons (1092), is thrown by Pandarus into Criseyde's bed and stripped by him 'al to his bare sherte' (1097–9). Who is to say if too much has been sacrificed to humour? If you create a clown, who is to say where the laughter should stop?

But there is, as always, more to it than a mere attributing to Chaucer's humour of what to some might look like a flaw. In the *Troilus* as elsewhere in Chaucer, the Knight's Tale or *The Parliament of Fowls* for example, love is seen both from within the situation and from outside it. Palamon and Arcite fight for the love of Emily in the forest of Theseus' country, where to be found by him is death. They are found by him, and they shall die, he says, till moved by the tears of Queen Hippolyta and Emily. The ladies see the pity of the situation as from within it, and he from outside sees the humour of it, but is touched by their tears and prayers, and therefore pardons Palamon and Arcite.[2] Till Nature bids them hold their tongue, the low birds comment impatiently

[1] I.ii.; ed. Scott, p. 275.
[2] *Canterbury Tales*, I (A) 1623–1825.

on the lack of procreative activity in true love as it is revealed in
the lofty speeches of the noble birds in *The Parliament of Fowls*
(379–525). The highest form of love poetry does not appeal to the
goose's party. The lesson is to be applied with some modification
to the love of Troilus.

The clowning of Pandarus balances the high rhetoric, but
should not, I think, be felt as destroying it. In the *Troilus*, as in
other poems by Chaucer, he creates situations fit for the lofty
verse he gives them. The high style of Troilus' languishing is
brought to earth by the tone of Pandarus:

> Yet Troilus for al this no word seyde,
> But longe he ley as stylle as he ded were;
> And after this with sikynge he abreyde,
> And to Pandarus vois he lente his ere,
> And up his eighen caste he, that in feere
> Was Pandarus, lest that in frenesie
> He sholde falle, or elles soone dye;
>
> And cryde 'Awake!' ful wonderlich and sharpe.
> 'What! slombrestow as in a litargie?
> Or artow lik an asse to the harpe,
> That hereth sown whan men the strynges plye,
> But in his mynde of that no melodie
> May sinken hym to gladen, for that he
> So dul ys of his bestialite?'
>   (1.722–35)[1]

If Chaucer had been writing wholly from within Troilus' love
agony, he would not have made Pandarus shatter the edifice of
woe built up through Troilus, and built up sufficiently for us to
see that he is writing of it with sympathy. Perhaps in some of the
moaning, Troilus may seem to indulge his affection too much,
though in literature the woe of love tolerates no moderation.
Chaucer offers a balanced diet of poetic gradations, with Troilus
in his sorrows, but also in his short-lived joys, at the top of the
scale together with Antigone's Trojan song, some of the narrative,

[1] For other Chaucerian uses of the cry 'Awake' see *Book of the Duchess*, 179–83,
House of Fame, 556–60, imitated in *The Kingis Quair*, st. 179.

and the end of the poem. The characterization and the action are subordinate, and if we look to characterization first we may bring to the poem the wrong values for judging Troilus—those of the goose's party. The balanced diet includes moments when for a brief time Troilus loses in broken accents the high rhetoric that is usually attached to him by Chaucer:

> But at the laste this woful Troilus,
> Neigh ded for smert, gan bresten out to rore,
> And with a sorwful noise he seyde thus
> Among hise sobbes and his sikes sore:
> 'Lo, Pandare! I am ded withouten more.
> Hastow nat herd at parlement,' he sayde,
> 'For Antenor how lost is my Criseyde?'
>   (IV.372–8)

That is only to make room for Pandarus' chatter; Troilus—voiceless as he appeared very briefly—finds his voice again and answers in twelve splendid stanzas (435–518). In Troilus' company Criseyde too can rise to longer flights of poetry than Chaucer usually thinks appropriate for her. If I am right in thinking that her words to Troilus near the beginning of her longest speech, that of encouragement when all seems lost (IV. 1254–1414), 'I am a womman, as ful wel ye woot' (1261), are a *double entendre*, Chaucer has undermined her grandest effort; and that is probably the purpose too of Chaucer's concluding assurance that Criseyde has spoken 'of good entente':

> And treweliche, as writen wel I fynde,
> That al this thyng was seyd of good entente;
> And that hire herte trewe was and kynde
> Towardes hym, and spak right as she mente.
>   (IV.1415–18)

These words inspire little confidence in her veracity, and prepare for the reception of her great vow to return on the tenth day (IV. 1528–96).

The last book is tragic reading to those that feel, and comic to those that think. A great range of poetic skills is attached to Troilus, in his *Canticus* and his *Littera* especially, and the tragic tone is depressed from near the beginning via Boccaccio by Ovid's old pillow:

> 'Wher is myn owene lady, lief and deere?
> Wher is hire white brest? Wher is it, where?
> Wher ben hire armes and hire eyen cleere
> That yesternyght this tyme with me were?
> Now may I wepe allone many a teere,
> And graspe aboute I may, but in this place,
> Save a pilowe, I fynde naught t'embrace.'
> (v.218–24)[1]

The glories of the last book, however, exceed the limitations of the poem's hero, in whose defence I write this paper.

As we look back over the *Troilus* the happiest memory is of that time at the end of the third book when Fortune led Troilus and Criseyde in joy, though even there the idyllic rhetoric is disturbed a little by Troilus' often taking the hand of Pandarus to whom he is indebted for his bliss (III.1737). In war there was none, 'Save Ector' (1775), who terrified the Greeks as much as did Troilus made nobler by love. In time of truce we see him hunting:

> In tyme of trewe, on haukyng wolde he ride,
> Or elles honte boor, beer, or lyoun—
> The smale bestes leet he gon biside.
> And whan that he com ridyng into town
> Ful oft his lady from hire wyndow down,
> As fressh as faukoun comen out of muwe,
> Ful redy was hym goodly to saluwe.
> (III.1779–85)[2]

Criseyde comes to him as fresh as falcon out of mew. In Boccaccio the image of the falcon is applied to Troilus—more appropriately, I think—when he lays aside for her the fierceness of the hunt and comes to her hand: 'And seeing Criseida at their trysts he assumes a pleasing and handsome face like a falcon unhooded' (III.91). That is how we should think of him, as well as on his couch of woe.

[1] See Robinson note on the last two lines; and cf. E. G. Stanley, op. cit. (page 100 fn. 1 above), p. 148.
[2] Cf. Robinson's note on III.1784.

VI

Thematic Interlace in
'The Canterbury Tales'

JOHN LEYERLE

ON THE surface *The Canterbury Tales* has a linear order like a string of beads; it is a collection of stories told by a group of travellers who meet by chance at the Tabard Inn and agree to tell one another stories on a pilgrimage to Canterbury. This is the obvious arrangement reported by Chaucer the pilgrim, but as Talbot Donaldson has convincingly shown,[1] this self-portrait is a fiction, not the poet. Chaucer the pilgrim, round of shape and short of wit, is one fictive author for a part of the poem, part of the fictive audience for the tales of the other pilgrims, and the one who reports all of what happens on the road to Canterbury. Like his description of the other pilgrims, his report of the simple, linear design of the sequence of tales is somewhat naïve because he mainly relates only outward appearances.

What Chaucer the pilgrim reports is the result of plans made by Harry Bailly, innkeeper of Southwark. As poet, Chaucer tends to treat members of the middle class with a degree of ironic amusement, or even mockery. A self-important publican who takes upon himself the uninvited role of guide for the pilgrimage, organizer of a tale-telling contest, and sole judge of the winner seems likely to be presented with some Chaucerian irony, and his opinions, especially his literary opinions, are to be taken uncritically only by the unwary. Under the circumstances, one may ask if Harry's literary plans are to be taken at face value as a guide to the poem's organization. To raise the question is to awaken doubt.

Although few readers take Harry's often ill-judged critical

---

[1] 'Chaucer the Pilgrim', *PMLA*, 69 (1954), 929-36. The article is reprinted in *Chaucer Criticism*, Vol. 1, *The Canterbury Tales*, ed. Richard J. Schoeck and Jerome Taylor (Notre Dame: University of Notre Dame Press, 1960), 1-13.

comments on individual tales seriously, most do accept his plan for a series of separate tales and concern themselves with the tales one by one. Studies of the poem as a whole tend to proceed tale by tale, each treated in a chapter of its own.[1] The individual tales are read to see how far each suits its teller dramatically, or how it relates to one or more tales, each taken as a unit. The Miller's Tale is read as a detailed *quiting* of the Knight's Tale, for example, and is seen to receive a *quiting* of its own in the Reeve's Tale. A view of the poem's order more complex than Harry's plan was inspired by one of the other forceful personalities of the pilgrimage, the Wife of Bath. In a pioneer study[2] G. L. Kittredge suggested that the theme of marriage bound four tales in close connection. The Clerk replies to the Wife of Bath and is followed, in turn, by the Merchant. The Franklin is seen to conclude the discussion. Yet Kittredge and those who have developed and refined his analysis of the Marriage Group show themselves still somewhat 'under the yerde' of Harry Bailly by treating the individual tales as discrete, self-sufficient units. Harry Bailly's arrangements do not account for the complicated interconnections of the Marriage Group; such complications in *The Canterbury Tales* as a whole are more extensive than has been widely recognized. Beneath the relatively simple, even naïve, surface structure of the innkeeper's poetics in which the tales are like beads on a string, is a very complex and intricate substructure. Chaucer the poet 'hadde moore tow on his distaf' than Chaucer the pilgrim and Harry Bailly recognize. The tales are connected by several thematic threads woven together to form the string that connects the tales together and provides interior coherence to the poem as a whole.

The object of this paper is to sketch briefly the way *The Canterbury Tales* as a poem, even in its unfinished state, is a

[1] For example, see Paul Ruggiers, *The Art of the Canterbury Tales* (Madison and Milwaukee: The University of Wisconsin Press, 1965), or Trevor Whittock, *A Reading of the Canterbury Tales* (Cambridge: University of Cambridge Press, 1968).

[2] *Modern Philology*, 9 (1911–12), 435–67. The article is reprinted in *Chaucer: Modern Essays in Criticism*, ed. Edward Wagenknecht (New York: Oxford University Press, 1959), 188–215 and in *Chaucer Criticism*, Vol. 1, ed. Schoeck and Taylor, 130–59.

knitting of a number of threads in complex patterns, a design which may be called thematic interlace. The term has the same basis in medieval aesthetics as does structural interlace,[1] but involves the weaving together of themes, not the disposition of narrative episodes as with structural interlace. Harry's plan is disjunctive by its nature; the thematic interlace is the underlying connective fabric of the text, the chief means by which Chaucer fashioned a loosely joined collection of tales into one poem. A design more complex than a sequence of tales operates as the horses amble down the road.

The thematic interlace of *The Canterbury Tales* has several threads of which four are considered here. These threads are found at irregular intervals in the text as they weave in and out of the various tales with labyrinthine complexity, but they all have their beginnings in the General Prologue and their endings in the Parson's Tale. Although the threads are here separated one by one for purposes of clarity, in the poem they combine and recombine with one another, and weave together in the fabric of the poem. The Parson contributes to the total design by tying up the threads, which is not at all the same as saying that his tale resolves the issues, even less that *The Canterbury Tales* is a poem that presents the human condition in terms of the seven deadly sins.[2] Although the Parson avoids Harry's request to tell a fable, he does follow his other request to 'knytte up wel a greet mateere'.

[1] For discussions of structural interlace, see John Leyerle, 'The Interlace Structure of *Beowulf*', *U.T.Q.*, 37 (1967), 1–17 and Eugène Vinaver, *Form and Meaning in Medieval Romance*, The Presidential Address of the Modern Humanities Research Association 1966 (Cambridge: Modern Humanities Research Association, 1966). Further analysis with useful bibliographical information on the subject can be found in Eugène Vinaver, *The Rise of Romance* (Oxford: Clarendon Press, 1971), especially chapter 4, 'The Poetry of Interlace', 68–98.

[2] For a detailed analysis supporting this observation, see Judson Boyce Allen, 'The old way and the Parson's way: an ironic reading of the Parson's Tale', *The Journal of Medieval and Renaissance Studies*, 3 (1973), 255–271. Allen's summary remark on positional significance is instructive; '. . . . the end of a work is not the emphatic place, and all our assumptions about story and climax, our presumption that pilgrimages exist in order to get somewhere—our automatic reaction to the fact that *The Canterbury Tales* is a narrative (of narratives) in imposing on it our notion of narrative climax—all this is wrongheaded and misleading.' p. 263.

Harry's request is in the tradition of the medieval poetics of interlace. In an important paper forthcoming in *Mediaeval Studies* Elizabeth Kirk discusses the importance of Robert of Basevorn's *Forma Praedicandi* as a theoretical statement on complex literary structure. Robert illustrates his analysis by dividing a sermon into nine parts: a1, a2, and a3; b1, b2, and b3; c1, c2, and c3. In Chapter 44 he discusses *circulatio* in which the first parts of each set of three are connected by linking them as follows: a1, b1, and c1; a2, b2, and c2; a3, b3, and c3. In Chapter 45 he discusses *convolutio* in which every part is linked with every other part. Robert ends this chapter with the remark, 'thus . . . all are interlaced, so that all and each correspond to each and all and thus interlaced enclose each other'.[1] Robert regards *circulatio* as more decorative than useful and *convolutio* as impossible for sermons, but the two chapters are a medieval description of the poetics of interlace and their importance as such had not yet been fully recognized. The Parson knits up *The Canterbury Tales* by linking his sermon to the themes that have been introduced before.

The subject of *The Parson's Tale* is penitence; but the bulk of his remarks concern the seven deadly sins. He concludes with the sin of *luxuria*, or lechery, the churchman's view of human sexuality that is one of the threads of the thematic interlace. The Parson knits up a thread, but its other end is in the General Prologue. Several of the pilgrims are described in terms of their sexual proclivities. The Squire is a hot-blooded young man whose elegant clothes, fine manners and chivalric efforts are 'in hope to stonden in his lady grace' (1,88).[2] The Monk loves *venerie*, a pun suggesting that the hunt is of both venison and Venus. The Friar's sexual appetites are described explicitly.

---

[1] Trans. Leopold Krul in *Three Medieval Rhetorical Arts*, ed. James J. Murphy (Berkeley, Los Angeles, and London: University of California Press, 1971), 196. For the text of the Latin, see Th.-M. Charland, *Artes praedicandi: contribution à l'histoire de la rhétorique au moyen âge*. Publications de l'institut d'études médiévale d'Ottawa, 7 (Paris and Ottawa, 1936).

[2] All quotations are from *The Works of Geoffrey Chaucer*, ed. F. N. Robinson, 2nd ed. (Cambridge: Houghton Mifflin, 1957) and are marked according to the line references in this edition.

> A FRERE ther was, a wantowne and a merye,
> A lymytour, a ful solempne man.
> In alle the ordres foure is noon that kan
> So muchel of daliaunce and fair langage.
> He hadde maad ful many a mariage
> Of yonge wommen at his owene cost.
>
> (1.208–13)

The social institution of sexuality, or marriage, is introduced in the description of the Wife of Bath and it proved to be a popular theme, especially among the secular members of the pilgrimage. The Knight starts his tale with a brief account of how Theseus subdued the Amazons in war and married their queen Ypolita. Most of the Knight's Tale concerns the wooing of Emelye by Arcite, supported by his patron Mars, and by Palamon, supported by his patron Venus, a suggestion that love often is presented in the poem as a mixture of aggression and desire. The Knight's Tale ends on a modestly hopeful note with the marriage of Emelye and Palamon. The Miller intervenes, however, with a tale of how human sexuality tends to escape the controlling bonds of marriage. The Miller's Tale has a poetic nucleus of holes in all their complex conjunctions: windows, doors, tubs, marlpits, rings, eyes, nether eyes, and towts; they reveal the anarchy and chaos of sexual licence in that wonderfully intricate tale.[1] The Reeve's Tale and the unfinished Cook's Tale also have sexuality as a central theme.

The theme of sexuality running through fragment I of *The Canterbury Tales* has the forms of courtship, marriage, and adultery, a tripartite pattern that occurs throughout the poem as a whole. The Man of Law's Tale is about the sexual trials and tribulations of Constance. The Clerk's Tale is less about marriage in terms of sexuality than of domination. The Merchant tells a bitter story of an old's man's passion for a young wife and her uninhibited infidelity in a pear tree. The Franklin's Tale presents a complicated view of the way sexuality is capable of causing generous treatment of other people. The Physician's Tale is a dark

---

[1] See John Leyerle, 'The Heart and the Chain', in *The Learned and the Lewed: Studies in Chaucer and Medieval Literature*, ed. Larry D. Benson, *Harvard English Studies*, 5 (1974), especially pp. 122–23.

view of the extremes to which lust can drive people. The Shipman's Tale treats the theme of sexuality mixed with the theme of gold. In The Nun's Priest's Tale Chauntecleer serves Pertelote and the other hens of the barnyard, 'Moore for delit than world to multiplye' (VII.3345); here, as in the Merchant's Tale, there are unmistakable suggestions of the fall of Adam and Eve in Paradise. The Manciple's Tale is an account of adultery and the dangers of telling unwelcome news.

What has been left out of this rapid summary is the most outspoken pilgrim on the subject of sexuality and marriage, the irrepressible Wife of Bath, whose account of her rich and varied sexual life constitutes one of the masterpieces of Chaucer's great poem. Her chief regret is not that she has lived an unconventional life transgressing the canons of respectability, but that she is growing old. In her tale an old woman subdues to her will a rapist and turns into a beautiful, faithful young girl in response to his vow of obedience to her. The Wife of Bath presents a remarkably able defence of her proclivities; her frank, humorous nostalgia is very disarming, but not for the Parson.

At the end of his account of the seven deadly sins he discusses lechery in words that respond to the Wife of Bath's arguments point by point and confute every statement she makes in her prologue in defence of her sexual behaviour and outlook. The Parson's remarks evidently apply to much of what has been told on the road to Canterbury. At the subsurface level of thematic interlace at least half of the tales are evidently concerned with sexuality, especially marriage. It is one of the pervasive themes of the poem and is far more extensive and complicated in The Canterbury Tales than the approach of Kittredge and his followers would indicate. The Parson's words are traditional moral theology and contribute to the views on sexuality in The Canterbury Tales but do not resolve them. One of the characteristics of interlace is that one point of the thread is as important to the whole design as another. It is a literary device that displays the complexities of issues in a way that makes resolution of the issues all but irrelevant. The Parson knits up the discussion of sexuality, but he does not resolve the complexities; they remain and always will.

He also knits up more than the theme of sexuality. He starts his account of *luxuria* by saying, 'After Glotonye thanne comth Lecherie, for thise two synnes been so ny cosyns that ofte tyme they wol nat departe' (x, 836). This is his transitional sentence following his account of *gula*, or gluttony, the Parson's theological term for immoderate consumption of food and drink, especially intoxicating drink.

> Glotonye is unmesurable appetit to ete or to drynke, or elles to doon ynough to the unmesurable appetit and desordeynee coveitise to eten or to drynke. This synne corrumped al this world, as is wel shewed in the synne of Adam and of Eve.
> (x.817–18).

The juxtaposition needs little explanation; it was something of a linguistic commonplace because of the pun on *Venus* and *vinum*, as the Wife of Bath remarks in connecting her sexual appetite to her consumption of wine,

> 'after wyn on Venus moste I thynke,
> For al so siker as cold engendreth hayl,
> A likerous mouth moste han a likerous tayl.'
> (III.464–66)

A similar connection is made in the Physician's description of the virtuous Virginia, 'wyn and youthe dooth Venus encresse' (VI. 59). In thematic interlace themes cross and weave together, touching and intersecting one another in patterns so complex that a full description of the connections is cumbersome. The reader must learn to perceive the connections for himself.

The theme of food and drink is introduced to the poem at its outset. *The Canterbury Tales* begin at the Tabard Inn in Southwark where Harry Bailly is innkeeper and host; he is in business serving food and, especially, drink. The pilgrimage begins at a pub, and is, according to Harry's plan, to end there. Several of the pilgrims are described in terms of their eating habits, notably the Prioress, the Franklin and the Summoner. The Miller started drinking early and is already drunk when the Knight finishes his tale. The five Townsmen, otherwise rather shadowy, take with them their own chef, a provision indicating that middle-class concerns about eating while travelling are by no means only a modern pre-occupation. Their cook has a taste for wine and by the time the pilgrims reach Bobbe-up-and-down he is so far in his cups that he falls off his horse. The Physician is much concerned with diet; he treats the complaints of his patients with drugs whose prescription apparently has as much to do with lucrative kickbacks from the apothecaries as with the cure of disease. The one unambiguously virtuous pilgrim concerned with food is the Ploughman, whose job is to grow crops for the rest of society. Nothing at all is said about his eating habits; here, as often, Chaucer's silences are significant.

Of the tales themselves the two that are particularly concerned with food and drink are the Pardoner's Tale and the Nun's Priest's Tale. The pilgrims stop while the Pardoner refreshes himself at a wayside inn before telling his tale; no doubt he does not drink alone. His tale contains a notable invective against gluttony, especially drunkenness, which is made not a little ironic by its setting in a pub. Like the situation of the Canterbury pilgrims as they listen to the Pardoner in an ale house, the tale begins in a tavern in Flanders; from there the three young *riotoures*, inflamed with drink, set out on the advice of an innkeeper (in the idiom of examination questions, compare and contrast Harry Bailly) to kill their enemy, death, who has slain one of their fellows. They learn from an old man that death will be found down a crooked way, under a tree. There they find 'wel ny an eighte busshels' (VI,771) of gold florins. The gold diverts their attention from their quest, although the object of their search, death, is nearer at hand than they realize. The youngest of the three is sent for bread and wine so that they can pass the day eating and drinking, waiting for night when they plan to carry the gold away unseen. He brings three bottles of wine, two of which are poisoned; his plan is to poison his fellows and keep all the gold himself, but he is killed by his two friends on his return. Their death follows swiftly from the poisoned wine. This last supper of bread and poisoned wine is evidently a parody of the eucharist, which is the only means of defeating death. The quest of the *riotoures* is more futile than they realize.

The Nun's Priest's Tale is centred around diet and eating. The 'povre wydwe, somdeel stape in age' (VII.2821), who rules the barnyard is described almost totally in terms of what she eats. After Chauntecleer has his frightening dream, Pertelote gives him elaborate advice on what he is to eat to cure the imbalance in his humours, which, as she claims, have caused his dreams. When Chauntecleer flies down from his beam he is caught by the fox, who means to eat him, just as he had eaten Chauntecleer's mother and father. The tale illustrates the law of diminishing fleas. The irony is not whether the rooster is to be eaten, but who is to do the eating. The poor widow wants the chickens as food; so does the fox. Chauntecleer is captured when he is pecking about eating on the ground, and his eye falls on a live delicacy for chickens, a butterfly which is, in turn, on top of a cabbage, its food but also food for the old woman. The nucleus of this tale is food and the inevitable violence that arises when the appetite for food is satisfied: beneath the humour is the stark reminder that we kill to eat.

The presiding figure of *The Canterbury Tales* is Harry Bailly, keeper of the Tabard Inn and dispenser of food and drink.

> Greet chiere made oure Hoost us everichon,
> And to the soper sette he us anon.
> He served us with vitaille at the beste;
> Strong was the wyn, and wel to drynke us leste.
> (I. 747–50)

He proposes the game of *The Canterbury Tales* in very explicit terms that involve the pilgrims in an agreement to return to the Tabard Inn at the end of the visit to Canterbury.

> And which of yow that bereth hym best of alle,
> That is to seyn, that telleth in this caas
> Tales of best sentence and moost solaas,
> Shal have a soper at oure aller cost
> Heere in this place, sittynge by this post,
> Whan that we come agayn fro Caunterbury.
> (I.796–801)

After all have agreed to the terms, the bargain is sealed with wine. All of this may seem an innocuous game, but there is an ominous undercurrent in the situation. The devil was often represented as an innkeeper[1] and *The Canterbury Tales* proceed from the Tabard, a type of Hell, to the cathedral at Canterbury, a type of Heaven, and back again, guided by the ambiguous figure of the Host. The devil has no intention of saving souls; yet he is, in effect, the guide of our earthly pilgrimage and his offerings of food and wine can be a dangerous deception.

Harry Bailly's plan for the pilgrims to return to the Tabard for 'a soper at oure aller cost' connects the theme of food and drink to the third major theme of the poem, gold. Harry Bailly, not surprisingly, has organized the expedition for his personal monetary gain. *One* pilgrim, at the end of the return journey, gets his dinner paid for jointly by all the other pilgrims back at the Tabard Inn. Harry Bailly, of course, gets the profits from the dinner and lodging for all; anyone who rebels against his critical judgements will have to pay the expenses on the road. Unlike the traditional guide of western literature, such as Vergil in the *Divine Comedy*, Scipio in the *Parliament of Fowls*, or the Eagle in the *House of Fame*, Harry Bailly takes his charges on a trip for his own profit, with a supper at the end; *oure Hoost* is a parody of the true Host[2] and offers a parody of the Last Supper.

In the General Prologue, a number of the pilgrims are described in terms of their interest in gold. The Prioress and the Monk have gold jewellery;[3] the Merchant engages in black-market activities

[1] The point is discussed by G. R. Owst, *Literature and Pulpit in Medieval England*. 2nd rev. ed. (Oxford: Basil Blackwell, 1961); see especially 92–7 and 434 ff.

[2] Fourteenth-century examples of the word *host* to mean the eucharist are, to judge from the citations in the *M.E.D.*, predominantly a Lollard usage. If so, Harry's remark of the Parson, 'I smelle a Lollere in the wynd' (II, 1173) is, as is usual with Chaucer, more complicated than it appears to be.

[3] These jewels can be seen as examples of the way small details reveal connections in the thematic interlace. The inscription on the brooch, *amor vincit omnia*, is usually translated 'love conquers all' with *vincit* taken from *vinco*, but *vincit*, taken from *vincio* also means 'binds', and the motto can equally well be translated, 'love binds all'. The idea of the binding of love is presented visually by the Monk's pin, which has a 'love-knotte in the gretter ende' (I, 197). The motto on one jewel is the same as the form of the other.

in currency; the Pardoner and the Monk misuse their ecclesiastical offices for private gain; the Sergeant of the Law twists the process for transmission of property to make gains for his clients and himself; the Physician works with the apothecaries to split the cost of expensive prescriptions; and the petty thefts of the Miller, the Manciple and the Reeve are of food and provisions, another example of the way thematic threads are woven together.

In its full development, passion for gold deforms the man it possesses. This is clearly seen in the Pardoner, who takes as his text *radix malorum est cupiditas* (1 Timothy, 6). His performance is adept at winning money. He is direct about his deceptions, which leads an unwary listener into thinking that he is being let in on a good thing; there is no better way to cheat a man than by an appeal to his avarice. The Pardoner's Prologue and Tale have some parallels with a medieval sermon, a situation that the Parson apparently does not miss. When he delivers his sermon at the end, he takes the very same text for his remarks on the sin of *Avaritia*.

> After Accidie wol I speke of Avarice and of Coveitise, of which synne seith Seint Paul that 'the roote of alle harme is Coveitise.' *Ad Thimotheum Sexto.* (X.739)

Just as the Parson's remarks on lechery apply to the Wife of Bath and answer her arguments point by point, so the Parson's remarks on avarice answer the Pardoner's arguments in his Prologue. The gold florins in the tale itself make the equation of gold and death apparent, even if it is never stated explicitly in the tale.

The Summoner's Tale is the story of an avaricious friar who hopes to win a rich bequest from a dying householder; his importunities are so offensive that he is given only flatulence; this unlikely bequest is the subject of a witty exercise in geometry which is a parody of the iconography of Pentecost.[1] Because of his covetousness, the friar receives fetid wind instead of the Holy Ghost, an indication of how far his corruption by avarice has gone.

[1] See Alan Levitan, 'The Parody of Pentecost in Chaucer's *Summoner's Tale*', *U.T.Q.*, 40 (1971), 236–46.

The Shipman's Tale is particularly interesting in the way the theme of gold is connected with the theme of sexuality. The story turns on the complex connections of the merchant of St Denis, his wife, and the monk who gains her sexual favours by giving her money he has borrowed from her husband. When the merchant asks the monk for repayment, he says he has paid the debt to the merchant's wife. This complex transaction involves the medieval view that the husband pays his *dette*, Latin *debitum*, to his wife in the sexual act.[1] The Latin word means what is owed and the monk plays with the words tail and tally to obfuscate the way he has played with the merchant's wife and gold. Although the jest is amusing, love has been put onto the gold standard, a usage which the Wife of Bath understood very well. She made each of her three old husbands give her property before she would allow him to 'paye his dette', a payment she then collected with a vigour that soon left her a widow. The notion of sexual activity as a *debitum* is a reminder of how easily love can turn to covetousness. The result is that human emotions such as those in the Knight's Tale are debased to a monetary transaction. Chaucer almost got to the subject of prostitution in the Cook's Tale, which seems to be moving in that direction when it breaks off.

The Canon's Yeoman's Tale also involves the same theme, man's vain desire to turn base metal into gold. The attempted transmutation is futile and the process only deforms its devotees into thieves. Trading on the avarice and gullibility of others, the alchemist is a stock figure of ridicule in the way he dupes himself by substituting gold for God as the object of his life and desires. In the process of transmutation the workers at the crucible become deformed into demons, blowing on the fire with soot-begrimed cheeks. The parody of creation is close because the crucible is shaped like a womb, constructed in hopes of begetting gold. The process is a vain attempt to imitate the creation of God, not for love, however, but for gold; *caritas* becomes *cupiditas*.

Where the theme of gold appears in *The Canterbury Tales* there

[1] For a discussion of the image patterns in the tale, see Janette Richardson, 'The Façade of Bawdry: Image Patterns in Chaucer's *Shipman's Tale*', ELH, 32 (1965) 303–13.

is relatively little of the comic animation that often accompanies the themes of sexuality and of food and drink. Although these two themes often enough show men and women behaving badly in the poem, they have a life-giving power and usually have redemptive aspects. A passion for gold, however, makes those possessed by it act badly. Consumed by materialism, they become insensitive to all but monetary gain; there is little life-giving power in gold. The Pardoner is so involved in getting money that he is unashamedly candid about his hypocritical frauds and describes himself with a chilling lack of human feeling.

> I preche of no thyng but for coveityse.
> Therfore my theme is yet, and evere was,
> *Radix malorum est Cupiditas.*
> Thus kan I preche agayn that same vice
> Which that I use, and that is avarice.
> (VI. 424–28)

The canon is so exasperated by his Yeoman's willingness to reveal his practice of fraudulent alchemy, that he rides off in an all but speechless rage. Harry Bailly is jolly about his pursuit of gold because he knows that commercial gaiety yields well if it is managed firmly. He stands to make money from the trip and sees to the arrangements in a loud and forceful manner, cynically using the various motives the pilgrims have for going to Canterbury. While the theme of gold in the poem shows a dark side of human nature, the themes of sexuality and of food and drink sometimes show the capacity of men and women to be moved by love, by *caritas* in theological terms. The theme of gold does not show this capacity for it limits men and women to possessive desire alone, *cupiditas*; as such, gold in *The Canterbury Tales* is closely associated with a fourth theme of the poem, death.

By the nature of literary interlace there are many instances where the themes of sexuality and of food and drink are woven together with that of death, but the connections with gold are markedly close. The theme of death has been glanced at several times before; it often weaves in and out of *The Canterbury Tales* and is so clear that brief discussion is sufficient here. Near the

opening of the Knight's Tale is the account of the heap of dead
bodies outside Thebes, in the middle of the tale is the description
of the temples of Diane, Mars and Venus in passages that read
like the fates of man, and near the end is the extended account of
the death and funeral of Arcite. In the Man of Law's Tale the
miraculous itinerary of Constance is strewn with the dead. The
Wife of Bath has buried five husbands and recalls the details with
a mortician's enthusiasm. The Friar tells a story of how close the
devil is at hand ready to take the unwary. The Physician tells a
gloomy tale of the way lust leads to the death of innocent as well
as of guilty. The Pardoner's Tale is about death itself which takes
the form of gold florins at the base of a tree; the Pardoner trans-
forms the metaphor of his biblical text, *radix malorum est cupiditas*,
into actuality and has the three young men experience death under
an actual tree of the seven deadly sins with actual gold at its roots.
Most of the episodes in the Monk's Tale involve death, but that
is the essence of tragedy. In the Nun's Priest's Tale the theme of
food and drink is woven with the theme of death because that is
what a barnyard is about; Chauntecleer's dream and his stories
about the way dreams foretell the future are about death as are
many of the Nun's Priest's digressions. Both the Prioress's Tale
and the Second Nun's Tale are about the death of martyrs, but
that is the essence of saints' lives. The Parson's sermon on penitence is an admonition that men and women should prepare themselves for death, which comes unannounced and uninvited. No
great literary sophistication is needed to realize that the road of the
pilgrimage to Canterbury is also the road of life that ends in
death. The prominence of the theme of death in *The Canterbury
Tales* may only reflect the fact that Chaucer was no longer young
as he composed the work; certainly mortal thoughts touch his
mind and fill his last words, the Retractions where all the masks
are gone and the poet faces death. *The Canterbury Tales* are full of
gaiety, life, and human vitality, and also full of the frailty of life,
the swiftness of time, and the certainty of death.

By nature of thematic interlace *The Canterbury Tales* is not
about any one strand of the design, but about all of them as they
are woven together. The meaning arises in some degree from the

linear course of the thematic threads, but Harry Bailly's literary arrangements have a commercial motivation and hardly get below the surface. Harry keeps time, measures distance on the road, and is content to keep the pilgrimage and the story-telling contest moving right along. In the underlying order of Chaucer's thematic interlace a relatively few threads weave back and forth to make the warp and woof of a tapestry, if the poem can be thought of as a text-textile, or word weaving. The tales are episodes depicted in the tapestry, but the threads that make a given episode extend to the other episodes and weave the fabric of the poem. This underlying order of thematic interlace, in contrast to Harry's plan, is atemporal and associative, synaesthetic and discontinuous, a manifestation of internal consciousness that extends beneath the surface order of distance and time, the order of Harry Bailly. Chaucer, as might be expected of him, is more complex and elusive than at first appears. The labyrinthine interconnections of threads defy full elucidation, so complex are the contrasts, juxtapositions, parallels, and tensions. The imagination and perception of the reader are free to move in all directions to make connections and find significance with few specific directions, or none, from Chaucer. This aspect of the thematic interlace accounts for a notable aspect of Chaucer's poetic genius, his great economy of statement; he can leave a given detail in very low definition that requires active participation from his audience or readers to supply the rest. The thematic interlace may also have contributed to the unfinished state of the poem; a few loose ends hardly matter and are probably unavoidable. The reader shares in the creation and does it by allowing all the parts of the threads to come together, consciously or not, in his own imagination until everything resonates at once. By comparison Harry Bailly's rough arrangements seem amateurish, and so they are. Beneath them Chaucer wove a thematic interlace of masterly design and put it so deep in the texture of his poem that most readers are content innocently to abide by Harry's rules, another—one supposes—of Chaucer's gentle, ironic jests.